ANIMALS, BIRDS and PLANTS

of the

BIBLE

By

WILLARD S. SMITH

Drawings by

WILLIAM DUNCAN

HODDER AND STOUGHTON

LONDON · SYDNEY · AUCKLAND · TORONTO

A

ADDAX. Several kinds of antelope were known in ancient Israel. One of the most common was the addax. It is about the size of a donkey, off-white in color except for its brown head. A short mane on the under side of the neck gives it the appearance of a large goat. It has a donkey-like tail, flat hoofs to keep it from sinking into the desert sand and long, thin, double-twisted horns, probably the most unusual of any animal.

ADDAX

Like other antelope, the addax was "clean" under the dietary laws and so was widely hunted. It is so fast that no dog can catch it. They are used, but falcons are usually a necessary part of the hunting team.

ADDER. See VIPER.

ADDER

AGAMID. A large lizard, often three feet in length, covered with scales and thornlike protrusions, the agamid presents a very frightening appearance. Actually it is harmless, living mainly on insects.

Though not mentioned by name in the Bible, the word "tortoise" in Leviticus 11:29 is now generally thought to be some kind of lizard, quite possibly the agamid.

AGAMID

ANT. The ant is one of the most common insects on earth. Solomon recognized its industry and skill in one of his familiar proverbs: "Go to the ant, thou sluggard; consider her ways and be wise." And in Proverbs 30:24,25 the wisdom of the ant is mentioned as one of the "four things which are little upon the earth, but they are exceeding wise: the ants are a people not strong, yet they prepare their meat in the summer."

The ability and skill of the ant in building a community of galleries and corridors underground was well known to the Hebrews.

ANT

AOUDAD. Also known as the "Barbary Sheep" the aoudad was quite common in Palestine, especially on and near Mt. Sinai. Today it is found only in the mountains of North Africa. It has large, smooth, wide-spread horns and a liberal display of "chin whiskers" which gives it a resemblance to a large billy goat. It is related to the Big Horn of the Rocky Mountains.

AOUDAD

APE

APE. The ape was not native to the Holy Land, but we read of the navy of Tharsish bringing King Solomon apes, along with "gold, silver, ivory and peacocks" on the long voyage from India and Ethiopia. (I Kings 10:22).

Since the ape, along with other kinds of monkeys, was highly prized in Egypt, the Hebrews were familiar with it.

ASP. See COBRA.

ASP

ASS. The ass, mentioned over 130 times in the Bible, was probably the most useful of all domestic animals to the Israelites. Because of its ability to thrive on a minimum of food, even a poor family might own an ass. It was used as a pack animal, for working in the fields and for transportation. Yet it was also a measure of wealth. Pharaoh's gift to Abraham was many asses. (Gen. 12:16). Job counted "five hundred she-asses" among his possessions (Job 1:3) which later (Job 42:12) had multiplied to "one thousand."

The ass of biblical times was a larger and more stately animal than the ass, or donkey, of today. It was usually tawny in color, the occasional white ass being greatly prized. Although once used in warfare, the horse superseded it in this capacity and the ass became a symbol of peace. Thus it was most fitting that the Prince of Peace should enter Jerusalem that first Palm Sunday riding on a lowly ass.

ASS

AUROCH (Urus). The huge auroch, or "urus," was also known as the "wild ox." Familiar to the Israelites, the animal was unknown to the translators of Hebrew scripture some 1500 years later. To them the many references to the very large horns of the animal (Deut. 33:17; Psalm 22:21; Isa. 34:7 et al) led these scholars to believe that the Hebrew writers referred to the unicorn. Hence "unicorn" in most references very likely should be "auroch."

Probably the auroch is the only "extinct" animal to be "re-created." The last known auroch died in Poland over 300 years ago. Zoologists, knowing much about the animal, reconstructed it by what might be called reverse cross-breeding of cattle believed to be ancestors of the auroch. Thus this huge animal of the far distant past, or a very close copy, lives again.

AUROCH

4

BABOON. The baboon is not mentioned in the Bible, and like the ape and other monkeys, it never lived in Palestine. Since it is quite likely that baboons were included in the exotic cargo brought to King Solomon's court from India and Africa, they may well have been known to the Hebrew people. Certainly the generations that lived in Egypt knew them, for the Egyptians looked upon the baboon with near reverence, sufficient reason for the Israelites to ignore the creature in their scriptures. However, some scholars believe that the word "peacock" in I Kings 10:22 should be translated "baboon."

BABOON

BARBARY SHEEP. See AOUDAD.

BADGER. See HYRAX.

BARBARY SHEEP

BASILISK. This fabulous creature, half snake and half cock, a product of a superstitious imagination, was "looked upon" with terror by many of the ancients. According to legend, the glance of the basilisk was sufficient to cause death. It was the symbol of the devil, a natural interpretation of Psalm 91:13, which in the Douay version reads, "thou shalt tread upon the adder and the basilisk."

BASILISK

BAT. We know the bat to be a flying mammal, but it is not strange that the ancient writers thought of it as a bird and so included it with the stork, the heron and the lapwing as "unclean" fowl. (Lev. 11:19.)

There are over a dozen species of bats in Palestine, living in caves and old buildings where they hang upside down through the day, flying out at night to frighten nervous humans, as is the case the world over. Isaiah, writing of "the day of the Lord," could think of nothing more degrading for the fate of the "idols of silver and gold" in "the last days" than that they be cast "to the moles and the bats." (Isa. 2:20.)

BAT

BEAR

BEAR. Though bears are now rare in Palestine, found only occasionally in the mountains of Lebanon, they were numerous in biblical times. The Syrian bear, indigenous to the area, may grow to six feet in length and weigh up to 500 pounds. It has a prominent forehead, short paws and long claws. As a cub it is dark brown, but as it matures it becomes a yellowish brown and in its old age it is a dirty white.

Though they rarely attack a person without provocation, they are extremely dangerous when aroused. Evidently Hushai knew this when he reminded Absalom that his father David and his followers were, when enraged, like "a bear robbed her whelps." (II Sam. 17:8.)

BEE

BEE. The bee is the smallest "domestic animal" in the world. Beekeeping was common in Egypt as far back as 4,000 B.C. Honey was used for embalming since it was the least expensive ingredient. And of course its food value was well known. The Hebrews evidently took their knowledge of beekeeping with them when they left Egypt since Ezekial lists honey as one of the chief exports of Judah. (Ezek. 27:17.) Some of this might well have been wild honey, for wild honeybees were, and are, common in Palestine. But it is quite certain that Palestinian farmers kept domestic honeybees, selling both honey and beeswax.

Evidence that the potency of an attack of angry bees was well known is found in Deuteronomy 1:44 and in Psalm 118:12. In both references the attack of enemies is likened to an attack by a swarm of bees.

BEHEMOTH

BEHEMOTH. Job's mention and description of "behemoth" (Job 40:15-24) has raised speculation among scholars as to just what animal he referred to. It was once thought that the elephant was meant. Now it is generally agreed that the description of its habitat, its great size and strength, its feeding and drinking habits best fit the hippopotamus. (Which see.)

The behemoth is the subject of many legends in Hebrew folklore, a mythical creature along with the unicorn and the cockatrice.

BOAR

BOAR, WILD. Though once common in Palestine the only mention of the wild boar in the Bible is in Psalm 80:13. It was a constant menace to farmers since a field of grain or a vineyard might be destroyed by wild boars in a single night. Since the boar is a wild pig, it was unclean by Mosaic law. Hence the farmer who killed the boars ravaging his crops did not have the compensation of using it for food.

It is interesting to note that in Albrecht Durer's painting, "The Prodigal Son," the swine with their tusks resemble the wild boar rather than the domesticated pig.

6

BUBAL. The bubal, or Hartebeest, is one of several species of antelope found in parts of the Middle East. The Arabs call it a "wild cow." In ancient times it lived in the arid regions of Egypt and probably as far as northern Arabia and into southern Palestine.

Since the bubal seems to have been the only animal of the deer or the antelope family to survive in these arid regions, this may have been the source of the venison that Esau brought to Isaac. (Gen. 25:28.) And the bubal would have been an important source of meat for the wandering Children of Israel.

BUBAL

BULL. Since cattle were an important factor in Hebrew living, the bull was a practical necessity. While the Israelites did not deify the bull as did the Egyptians with their bull-formed god Apis, and the Babylonians who worshipped the winged bull-god, some of this obeisance found its way into Hebrew religious literature. A literal translation of "the Mighty One" (Gen. 49:24; Isa. 1:24) is "Bull of Jacob (Israel)". Horns of the bull adorned the top of the altar in King Solomon's temple (I Kings 7:44), a practice condemned by the later prophets.

BULL

BUTTERFLY. While butterflies are not specifically mentioned in the bible it is quite possible and even probable that in some instances the ancient writer had butterflies in mind when "moths" are mentioned. Certainly they must have been common. One can easily imagine the boy Jesus chasing butterflies in the fields around Nazareth on a summer day, the gossamer beauty of these frail creatures reminding him that the least of his Father's creations was a thing of enchanting beauty.

BUTTERFLY

C

CALF. Besides reference to the calf as a young cow, it is mentioned many times in the Bible in other connections. Probably the best known is the incident of the Golden Calf which Aaron had made for the Children of Israel to worship. (Ex. 32.) Nor were the Hebrew people ever allowed to forget their idolatrous transgression which so aroused the wrath of Moses. The Golden Calf is cited by the psalmist (Ps. 106:19; by the prophet Hosea, Hos. 8:6), and in the New Testament by Stephen (Acts 6:39-41) in his eloquent speech just before his death.

A young calf was deemed an appropriate sin offering.

CALF

CAMEL

CAMEL. The camel is one of the first animals mentioned in the Bible. The fact that it could go for days without water and with little food; its ability to scent water before an oasis was sighted; its stamina and, when necessary, its speed—a camel can outrun a horse—made it of great importance to the Israelites. The species used was the single-humped dromedary.

Not only was the camel important as a means of transportation, but it was also much used as a work animal. Its milk, along with butter and cheese, were important items in the Hebrew diet. Cloth was made from its hair (Matt. 3:4), its hide was tanned for leather, and the dried dung was used as fuel and as an ingredient in roofing.

CAT

CAT. The cat is not mentioned in the Bible. The Israelites looked on it with contempt. This may have been due to the fact that the Egyptians, their masters for generations, worshipped the cat, and to kill one was a crime punishable by death. When a cat died the Egyptians often embalmed it and buried it in an ornate coffin. Such pagan animal worship must have galled the Hebrews and made the cat dispicable. And this attitude was probably hardened long after when their later captors, the Babylonians, kept cats in the sacred places of the temple. Yet, in spite of this general feeling, it is quite probable that the cat was a household pet among the Israelites of a later date.

CATERPILLAR

CATERPILLAR. Since moths, grasshoppers and butterflies were common in Palestine, caterpillars were familiar. They are mentioned many times in the Bible, often when pestilence is the theme (I Kings 8:37; Psalm 78:46; Isa. 33:4), giving the impression that the writers made no definite distinction between the wormlike larvae of insects found in refuse and the fussy innocent caterpillars of, e.g. butterflies. But no doubt the Hebrews were aware of the wonder of the metamorphosis of the egg-larvae-flying insect cycle.

CENTAUR

CENTAUR. Whether or not the people of the Bible knew of the centaur we cannot be certain. It is quite likely they did believe in this mythical creature that has come down through the ages—in imagination. It was supposed to have the head and torso of a man and the body of a horse. Symbolically it represented man divided against himself, torn between good and evil.

CHAMELEON. The chameleon was as familiar to the ancients as it is to people today. Its unique ability to change its color, not so much to match the background as a means of camouflage, but because of the temperature and its emotions, is well known. A most peculiar characteristic of the chameleon is its eyes. Each eyeball can move independently, thus giving the wierd effect of the animal looking two ways at once—which actually it does! The chameleon is harmless, its diet consisting mostly of insects which it traps with a quick jab of its long tongue.

CHAMELEON

CHAMOIS. The Hebrew word translated "chamois" in Deuteronomy 14:5 is the broad description of "antelope" and might refer to any one of several species. While there is a remote variety of chamois native to Asia Minor it is doubtful if the true chamois ever lived in the Holy Land. The Barbary Sheep might be the animal intended in the Deuteronomy passage.

CHAMOIS

CLAM. Since clams, along with other marine animals that have no fins or scales were classed as unclean in the Mosaic dietary ruling, they were not used as food by the Israelites. But they must have been known to the inhabitants of the seacoast towns.

CLAM

COCKATRICE. It would do no good to look up the cockatrice in a nature book: there never has been such an animal. Mention of it in several bible passages of early translations (Isa. 11:8; 50:5; Jer. 8:17) was logical to the English translators to whom the cockatrice—a kind of serpent hatched from a chicken egg—was a generally accepted creature, even though never seen. Later translators have changed this mythical "animal" into the very real "adder," as do footnotes in the King James passages.

COCKATRICE

CONEY

CONEY. See HYRAX.

CORAL

CORAL. Whether the Hebrews realized that coral, abundant in the sea waters of the Middle East, is the skeleton remains of tiny animals is questionable. But the wealthy used it in decorating their homes, particularly the red coral. Possibly this is what Job had in mind when he reminded Bildad the Shuhite that "no mention shall be made of coral or crystal" in setting a price on wisdom. (Job 28:18.) Ezekial's inclusion of coral with "emeralds, fine linen and agate" (Ezek. 27:16) indicates that it was considered a valuable commodity.

CRICKET

CRICKET. Translation of the Hebrew word as "beetle" in the King James version of the Bible (Lev. 11:22) is changed to "cricket" in the Revised version, leaving us uncertain as to just what member of the grasshopper family was meant. In any case we can be quite sure that the chirp of crickets, made by the cricket rubbing its hind legs together, was as familiar to the people of Bible times as it is today.

CROCODILE

CROCODILE. Even though the crocodile is not mentioned in the Bible it must have been known to the Children of Israel because of their long sojourn in Egypt where it was, and still is, plentiful. Since the Egyptians worshipped the crocodile as one of their gods, we can be sure the animal was abhorrent to the Israelites.

Some scholars believe that the crocodile once inhabited the Jordan River and the swamps of northern Israel.

D

DEER, FALLOW

DEER, FALLOW. The Fallow Deer, a small animal only about 3 feet high, lived only in northern Palestine. Some scholars believe a species of antelope was referred to in, e.g. Deuteronomy 14:5 where the fallow deer is mentioned with the hart. This is not a repetition as the hart is the male of the Red Deer.

DEER, RED

DEER, RED. The Red Deer, a relative of the North American elk, was plentiful in the Holy Land. As mentioned above, the male Red Deer is called the Hart: "As the hart panteth after the water brooks" (Ps. 42:1) is a graphic word picture of a tired, thirsty male deer. The psalmist continues, "so panteth my soul after thee, O God."

DOG. To the Hebrews of biblical times, as to most eastern people except the Egyptians, the dog was an outcast, a scavenger to be despised. It is referred to over forty times in the Bible and from Deuteronomy 23:18 where it is "an abomination," to Jesus' admonition, "Do not give that which is holy unto the dogs," this "abomination" is evident. The pariah dogs, belonging to no one, ran in packs, roaming and howling at night, subsisting on refuge and even ravaging human corpses. However, the Jews learned that dogs could be trained to warn of wild animals and thieves. Job speaks of "the dogs of my flock." (Job 30:1.) This could have been a type of shepherd dog somewhat similar to the ones we know today. But the dog was seldom a household pet. And even today the worst of insults in the eastern countries is to call a person a dog.

DOG

DOLPHIN. The playful dolphin is one of the swiftest and strongest of fish. Some early writers believed the "big fish" in the story of Jonah's harrowing experience to be a dolphin. But the physical makeup of the dolphin readily dispenses this suggestion. In Christian art it has often been used to symbolize salvation and resurrection.

DOLPHIN

DONKEY. See ASS.

DRAGON. All ancient peoples believed in dragons. They are mentioned several times in the Bible, quite often as symbolic of evil forces, as in Psalm 91:13— "The young lion and the dragon shalt thou trample underfoot." Ezekial could have been referring to the crocodiles of the Nile when he wrote of "the great dragons that lie in the midst of the rivers." (Ezek. 22:33.) Just how the "real" dragons were pictured is difficult to say, but there was no doubt as to their sinister character.

DONKEY

DRAGON

DUGONG. (SEA COW). The dugong, a specie of sea cow, is found in the Indian Ocean and in the Red Sea. Hence it was known to the Hebrews. It is one of nature's strangest creatures: a mammal, as the alternate name of "sea cow" implies, but living mostly in the water like a seal, which it somewhat resembles. Its hide makes excellent leather of a bluish tinge and no doubt was used by the Israelites.

DUGONG

E

EEL

EEL. Eels were found in the local lakes of Palestine, and the salt water variety in the Mediterranean. Since they have neither scales or fins their use as food was forbidden under the prescribed dietary law. (Lev. 11:10.) It is quite possible that "eel" instead of "serpent" was used by Jesus when he asked, "If (his son) asks for a fish, will he give him a serpent?" (Matt. 7:10.) An eel would be more familiar, and as worthless to a hungry Israelite as a stone.

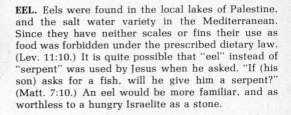

ELEPHANT

ELEPHANT. Though there is no direct reference to the elephant in the Bible, ivory is mentioned often. A symbol of great wealth, it was one of the wonders of King Solomon's temple. Since the main source of ivory was the tusks of the elephant the Hebrews must have known of this huge animal even though they never saw one. It is interesting to note that the Hebrew word for ivory is almost the same as that of southern India and Ceylon.

The Asiatic elephant once lived much closer to the Mediterranean than it does today. When Egypt conquered Syria about 1460 B.C. a herd of war elephants was part of the army.

EWE. The female sheep was often a household pet of the Hebrews as indicated in Nathan's story in II Samuel 12:1-6. It was seldom used for food or for sacrificial purposes for the very practical reason that the ewe was the mother of the next generation.

EWE

F

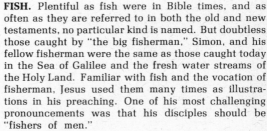

FISH. Plentiful as fish were in Bible times, and as often as they are referred to in both the old and new testaments, no particular kind is named. But doubtless those caught by "the big fisherman," Simon, and his fellow fisherman were the same as those caught today in the Sea of Galilee and the fresh water streams of the Holy Land. Familiar with fish and the vocation of fisherman, Jesus used them many times as illustrations in his preaching. One of his most challenging pronouncements was that his disciples should be "fishers of men."

The letters of the Greek word for fish, **ichtys,** are the first letters of the words of the Greek phrase, "Jesus Christ, Son of God, Saviour." Hence the fish was one of the earliest symbols of Christianity.

FISH

FLEA. The pestiferous flea was doubtless as much of a nuisance to the ancients as it is today. Certainly the unsanitary conditions common in ancient times would have made it a common pest. The only direct reference to the flea in the Bible is by David who chides Saul and successfully seeks to appease him by reminding the king that he is wasting his strength seeking "a flea as one doth hunt a partridge in the mountains." (I Sam. 26:20.)

FLEA

FLY. Flies swarming over the land are listed as the fourth plague that ravished Egypt. (Ex. 8:24.) They are one of the most widely distributed of insects, as prevalent thousands of years ago as now, and of many varieties. The common housefly was a pest, but equally so were the "botfly," or "gadfly," which deposits its eggs in the fur of a cow or other animal. (Jer. 46:20.) The tsetse fly, carrier of the germ of "sleeping sickness," was familiar to the Hebrews in Egypt.

FLY

FOX. The Red Fox was the most common in Bible lands, but the smaller Egyptian Fox, rust-colored with a white belly, was prevalent in southern Palestine. The shiny golden colored Syrian Fox was common in the northern forests. The fox has always been noted for its craftiness and cunning: Jesus referred to Herod as "that fox" (Luke 13:32). And rather pensively he reminds his disciples that "foxes have holes . . . but the Son of Man hath not where to lay his head." (Matt. 8:20.)

In the Song of Solomon (2:15) mention is made of "the little foxes that spoil the vines" of the vineyard. Foxes like the sweet juice of the grapes, and also they burrow tunnels in the vineyards that destroy the roots of the vines.

Samson's "300 foxes" (Judges 15:4) more likely were jackals, which see.

FOX

FROG. Not only were frogs abhorrent to the early Israelites and "unclean," but the fact that their Egyptian masters paid obeisance to the frog god Hequet made the creature even more despicable.

Frogs of many species were common in Egypt. The plague of frogs, second of the ten, is described in detail in Exodus 8:1-14. The psalmist reminds the Children of Israel of this event in Psalms 78:45 and 105:34. The only other time the frog is mentioned in the Bible is in Revelation 16:13 when John tells of seeing "three unclean spirits like frogs."

FROG

G

GAZELLE

GAZELLE. The gazelle is common in Palestine today. It is a member of the antelope family, especially noted for its graceful body and movements. It is one of the fastest of animals, leaping as much as 3 feet in the air as it runs. Very shy, it travels in herds of 40 or 50. It is hunted for food but its speed make special techniques necessary for the hunter. The animals are sometimes driven into narrow valleys where they can more easily be shot. Sometimes they are captured in nets, or driven into pitfalls. The Egyptians made pets of the gazelle.

GECKO

GECKO. The gecko has always been a common type of lizard in the Holy Land. The difficulty of the early translators is evident in the translation of the name in Leviticus 11:30, where listed among the unclean "creeping things," is the "ferret." But there have never been ferrets in Palestine. Later scholars concluded that the correct name was "gecko."

There is an old superstition that a gecko walking on one's body causes leprosy. Even today many Arabs believe that it poisons all it touches. Actually it is harmless, though rather repulsive in appearance.

GNAT

GNAT. "Ye blind guides, which strain at a gnat and swallow a camel!" (Matt. 23:24.) So Jesus, in strong hyperbole, indicates that he is familiar with the pestiferous gnat. It was a common practice to strain wine through cloth to remove insects and foreign matter. Hence Jesus' illustration was easily understood, effectively ridiculing the hypercritical legalism of the Pharisee's religious practices.

While the King James version lists lice as the third of the plagues to beset Egypt, all other translations list gnats. Perhaps there would be little choice!

GOAT. The goat of the Hebrews was probably the species with long, floppy ears and covered with long, black silky hair. Both male and female had horns, but the male had an additional ornament of chin whiskers. It was an important domestic animal, providing meat, hair for weaving into cloth, hide for water bags, and even horns for trumpets. The skin was also used for the strings of the "nebal," a large harp, and for drum heads.

In addition to the above practical uses, the male goat was acceptable as a sin-offering. On the Day of Atonement one was chosen by chance. After the high priest had symbolically transferred the sins of the people to the goat it was turned loose in the wilderness. (Lev. 16:20-22.) We still refer to a "scapegoat" as one who bares the blame for others.

Both goats and sheep grazed in the same pasture but since the male goat was often ill-tempered toward the sheep, the flocks were kept separate. Hence Jesus' remarks in Matthew 25:32 . . . ". . . as a shepherd divideth his sheep from the goats."

GOAT

GRASSHOPPER. Many varieties of grasshopper are found in the Holy Land, probably the same ones that were common in ancient times. The locust, as the most destructive, is mentioned most often. But the name is also applied to crickets and katydids, especially when the reference is to something other than the havoc wrought by herds of locusts.

GRASSHOPPER

H

HAMSTER. This small rodent is found in the Middle East but is most common in Syria where it is a source of food for the Arabs. The Syrian hamster is somewhat smaller than the common pet, with a longer tail and silky hair of a golden color. It has large cheek pouches into which it stuffs food to be taken to its nest, burrowed as much as feet in the ground. Each animal occupies its own "quarters" consisting of a storage chamber and a "living room."

HAMSTER

HARE. The hare, and its close relative, the rabbit, are common to practically all of the temperate regions of the world. Two varieties of the hare are found in Palestine. One lives in the wooded inhabited areas, the other somewhat smaller species is found in the more barren regions.

Because of the ignorance of the times, the hare is classed as unclean "because he cheweth the cud." (Lev. 11:6.) However, neither the hare nor the rabbit is a ruminant. But the peculiar way they have of moving their lips — with which every child with a rabbit as a pet is familiar — does give the impression of cud chewing. On this presumption it was classed as "unclean" and not to be eaten.

HARE

HART

HART. As mentioned under "DEER," which see, the hart is the male of that species. It was used for food and it might well have been a hart which Isaac bade Esau hunt that he might have venison. (Gen. 27:3ff.)

HIND. The hind is the female of the Red Deer. Its use as food was forbidden. This was not for dietary reasons, but because the female was the bearer of the next generation.

HIND

HIPPOPOTOMUS (Behemoth). This, one of the largest of animals, would have been known to the Israelites during their long sojourn in Egypt where it was found in and near the Nile River. Job's reference to the behemoth (which see) (Job 40:15) probably was to the hippopotomus.

The young are born under water and can swim before they can walk. They weigh up to a ton when full grown. Job saw this huge creature as a demonstration of the creative power of God. Eaten by the Egyptians, the flesh was "unclean" to the Israelites.

HIPPOPOTOMUS

HORNET. There are at least four species of hornets in the Holy Land. The most common is the large yellow and reddish brown variety armed with the familiar poisonous sting of all hornets. Apparently they were as vicious in Bible times as today. Whether the promise of God to use hornets as one means of combating the enemies of Israel (Ex. 23:28) was meant literally or figuratively, its meaning is plain. (Joshua 24:12.)

HORNET

HORSE. Though mentioned often in the Bible—over 150 times—the horse never took the place of the lowly ass in the life of the Hebrews. Its use was mostly that of a war animal, vividly described as such by Job. (Job 39:19-25.) First to draw chariots—Solomon had 1400 (I Kings 10:26)—but later as cavalry. (Ezek. 38:15.)

For a long time Mosaic law forbade the breeding of horses (Deut. 17:16) and they were imported from Egypt. But when the superiority of the horse in warfare became apparent, this law was conveniently overlooked. We do not know the breed of horses common in Palestine, but it was probably the rather small, swift animal common in Egypt. The large Arabian horse was not known at that time.

HORSE

HYENA. The hyena was probably the most detested animal of the ancient world, due largely to its habit of digging up graves. Absalom was buried under a pile of stones to prevent this from happening to his corpse. (II Sam. 18:17.) It was also the subject of many superstitions: its scent was believed to corrupt the air; sandals and leggings made of its hide were said to be protection against hynea bites. Once plentiful in Palestine the striped hyena is now rare. Strange as it seems, young hyenas are said to be easily tamed and the Egyptians kept them as pets. Also as a source of food.

HYENA

HYRAX (Coney). Probably the most familiar reference to the hyrax, or coney as it is more commonly known, is Psalm 104:8: "The high hills are a refuge for the wild goats and the rocks for the coneys." The translation, "badger" in the Revised Version is misleading since the badger is unknown in Palestine. The hyrax resembles a large rodent and is sometimes called a "desert rat." It has a thick body covered with fine fur, short legs, a very short tail and small, round ears. A marked peculiarity of the hyrax is the formation of its feet. There are skin folds between the toes. Glands on the bottom of the feet keep them moist and so provide a suction effect, most helpful to the animal as it climbs the sheer rocks among which it lives in colonies of up to fifty. It is a shy creature, its safety depending largely on its ability to scamper into rock crevices on a warning signal from stationed "lookouts."

HYRAX

Strange as it seems, zoologists believe that the hyrax is a survivor of an ancient type of hoofed animal, its nearest living relative being the elephant, or possibly the Sea Cow!

I

IBEX. While the ibex is not mentioned by name in the Bible, most naturalists believe the "wild goat" refers to this animal. Traveling in herds of 8 or 10, it lived high in the craggy mountains where sure-footedness and agility were essential. It is still found in Palestine.

When David and his followers were fleeing from the wrath of Saul, ibex may have been their main food supply "in the wilderness of En-gedi." (I Sam. 24:1.) En-gedi was known as the "fountain of goats," quite possibly ibex.

IBEX

J

JACKAL

JACKAL. A bushy-tailed relative of the dog, the jackal is still common throughout the lands of the Bible. It was unknown to the English translators. "Fox" was the nearest they could come to identifying the animal from the Hebrew description. It is very likely that the 300 "foxes" which Samson caught, tied tail to tail, and turned loose as living firebrands to destroy the crops of the Philistines, were jackals. (Judges 15:4.) Foxes travel alone and capturing 300 would be almost impossible. But jackals, traveling as they do in packs, would have made the capture of so large a number more plausible.

JELLYFISH

JELLYFISH. The jellyfish is found in the Mediterranean Sea and the Indian Ocean, so would have been known to the Israelites living near the seacoast, but it is not mentioned in the Bible.

JERBOA. The jerboa is a rodent, somewhat larger than the rat, common to much of the Middle East. Its hind legs are five or six times longer than the front, giving it a kangaroo look and, in fact, enabling it to leap like a small knagaroo so effectively that it can "run" faster than a man. It has rabbit-like ears, large eyes and is covered with a soft, sandy-colored fur except for its white belly and a black and white tassel at the end of its tail. It feeds on plants and insects. It lives in burrows made in the hard, sandy soil and, being very shy, is seldom seen.

JERBOA

K

KERMES

KERMES. It is difficult to think of the kermes as an "animal" in any category. It is a nodelike insect, about the size of a pea, found on the kermes oak. The dried bodies of the female, today as in ancient times, are treated with vinegar to make a scarlet dye that will not bleach or fade. This is the "scarlet" referred to in the Bible. Its permanence is what Isaiah refers to when he promises that "though your sins be as scarlet they shall be white as snow." (Isa. 1:18.) This scarlet dye was very expensive and only the wealthy could afford garments of scarlet. Still, soldiers were often attired in scarlet. It was a scarlet robe that the soldiers placed on Jesus (Matt. 27:28).

L

LEECH. The leech ("blood sucker") has not changed through the centuries. Its flat body is up to 5 inches long with suction pads at either end. It has three knifelike projections of its mouth with which it pierces the skin to suck the blood of its host. No doubt it was as repulsively familiar in Jesus' time as it is today. It is the only true worm mentioned in the Bible where it is referred to as the "horseleach." (Prov. 30:15.)

LEECH

LEOPARD. The derivation of the English name "leopard" is interesting. When first discovered by early European travelers, to whom such an animal was unknown, they thought it a cross between a lion and a panther. So they combined the Latin word for each: "leo" (lion) and "pard" (panther).

The leopard was well known in Bible times, especially in the forested regions of Lebanon where its swiftness and ferocity made it a constant menace to grazing flocks. It is one of the animals Isaiah mentions in his word picture of peace (Isa. 11:6). And Jeremiah indicates the familiarity of the people with the animal when he asks, "can . . . the leopard change his spots?" (Jer. 13:23).

LEOPARD

LEVIATHAN. The ancient beliefs of the Hebrews in the field of nature coincided with those of other races in regard to strange and mythical creatures such as the unicorn, the cockatrice—and the leviathan. While Job might have been describing a crocodile in Job 41 where the word "leviathan" is used, his people believed it to be a large sea monster about which there were many fantastic legends. One such legend was that the leviathan was not capable of reproducing lest they crowd all other creatures out of the ocean! The psalmist pictures it as a playful animal. (Psalm 104:26.) In Isaiah 27:1 it is a serpent-like creature. Modern scholars are inclined to think that these and other references are to a mythical dragon.

LEVIATHAN

LICE. Human lice were as numerous among the ancients as among modern man where unsanitary conditions existed. Not only does the bite of the louse cause extreme itching, but the insect is the carrier of diseases, especially cholera and typhus. Human lice are of two kinds, head and body. Strangely, each stays pretty much in its own territory!

Plant lice of many species are older than civilization. The plague of lice was the third of the ten plagues to strike Egypt. (Ex. 8:17.)

LICE

LION

LION. The lion, ensign of the tribe of Judah, is the most mentioned wild animal in the Bible. It was probably the relatively small Persian lion, a species native to the Middle East. Though ferocious by nature and much feared, tamed lions were pets at the courts of the Pharaohs, and later of King Solomon. Untamed, they were also kept in pits ("dens"). Into one of these "dens" Darius, king of Persia, cast Daniel.

The lion is used in the Bible as a symbol of strong spiritual qualities: "the righteous are as bold as a lion" (Prov. 28:1); as symbol for God: (Isa. 31:4); and, by contrast, the devil is likened to a "roaring lion . . . seeking whom he may devour." (I Peter 5:8.)

LIZARD

LIZARD. There are many kinds of lizards in the Holy Land. Unfortunately the early writers of the scriptures, and later the translators, were very ambiguous in their references to them. The sand lizard very likely was the "snail" mentioned in Leviticus 11:30 and Psalm 58:8, an example of the difficulty in establishing individual identity. Common in the area were the agamid, the chameleon, the gecko, which see.

Less common than the other varieties was the "land crocodile," some 3 feet in length, its body covered with green and yellow spots and with golden rings around its neck. The Nile Monitor, common to Egypt as its name implies, grows up to 6 feet in length. It, too, most have been known to the Hebrew people.

LOBSTER

LOBSTER. The lobster is a marine animal and was eaten by the Egyptians and other maritime neighbors of the Israelites. But to them it was "unclean" and apparently they considered it of no importance. It is not mentioned in the Bible.

LOCUST

LOCUST. The locust, plague of the Middle East since earliest times, is a species of grasshopper. It is about 2 inches long, reddish brown and yellow, with a wingspread of nearly 5 inches. In early or mid-summer hordes of them, borne on the prevailing winds, begin the destructive migration. The result is as devastating today as it was when the plague of locusts visited Egypt. (Ex. 10:13-15.)

The Mosaic dietary law permits the eating of locusts. While the locusts which John the Baptist subsisted on in the wilderness (flavored with honey) could have been the insect, it is also possible that the reference (Matt. 3:4) is to the fruit of the carob tree, which see.

M

MAGGOT. The maggot, larval stage of the fly, is as well known as the fly itself. In most cases biblical writers have used the word "worm" in referring to maggots. "They shall lie down alike in the dust, and the worms shall cover them." (Job 21:26.) Dead bodies are inferred here which earthworms would not molest but which would soon be covered with maggots. The loathsomeness of the maggot is manifested in the taunting challenge to the king of Babylon: "Thy pomp is brought down to the grave . . . the worm is spread under thee, and the worms cover thee." (Isa. 14:11.)

MAGGOT

MOLE. The mole is listed among the unclean animals in Leviticus 11:30. And Isaiah (2:20) speaks of man's idols being cast "to the moles and the bats." Doubtless the mole was familiar to the Hebrew people, but "mole" might also mean the mole rat, which see.

MOLE

MOLE RAT. Though not mentioned in the Bible the mole rat was and is common in Palestine. This leads us to believe that the word translated "mole" in some cases refers to the mole rat. It has much the same habits—burrowing into the ground, feeding on roots and bulbs. It has the same general shape as the mole, though much larger. It, too, has almost sightless eyes and is covered with soft, thick gray fur.

MOLE RAT

MONKEY. Though not found anywhere in biblical lands, monkeys, particularly the baboon, which in Egypt was considered sacred to the god Thoth, were known to the Hebrew people because of their long sojourn in Egypt. As mentioned under "APES," several species of primates were common in the court of King Solomon, brought from Africa and India.

MONKEY

MOSQUITO. There is no doubt but what the Hebrew people were acquainted with the pestiferous mosquito, including the "anophles," carrier of malaria and yellow fever germs. The Hebrew word translated "mosquito" is not too clear but we can be sure the buzzing and their bites were well known. In fact, a kind of mosquito netting is mentioned in the apochraphal book of Judith where the author mentions one "with purple and gold and emeralds and precious stones."(!) (Judith 10:21.)

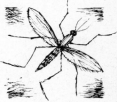

MOSQUITO

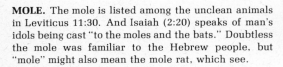

MOTH

MOTH. Probably the most familiar quotation concerning the moth is the admonition of Jesus: "Lay not up for yourselves treasures on earth where moth and rust corrupt . . ." (Matt. 6:19). As every housewife who stores winter clothing in cedar chests and moth balls knows, it is the larvae of the clothes moth, not the adult, which does the damage. Evidently the ancients also had this problem. Job states it definitely when he cries out bitterly, "He (man) as a rotten thing, consumeth, as a garment that is moth eaten." (Job 13:28.) There were other kinds of moths, but only the clothes moth is mentioned in the Bible.

MOUSE

MOUSE. There are over twenty varieties of mice in the Holy Land. The Hebrew word **akbar** is used which was a generic term applying to all species. The Mosaic prohibition against their use as food indicates that the people were familiar with them. (Lev. 11:29.) Prominence that seems out of proportion to their size is given the mouse in I Samuel 6. As a guilt offering for their theft of the ark, and which they later decided to return, they were instructed to bring to the Israelites "five golden mice" (I Sam. 6:4) representing the five Philistine lords.

MULE

MULE. The mule is mentioned 22 times in the Bible, but only in the Old Testament. And only once before King David bade Solomon ride to him on a mule. The breeding of mules, a male donkey mated with a female horse, resulting in an always sterile offspring, was forbidden by Mosaic law. (Lev. 19:19.) But mules became so important to the Israelites that this law was often disregarded. Mules, combining the size and strength of the horse (which see) with the sure-footedness of the donkey, became popular as a war animal, as a beast of burden, and as a riding animal for royalty. (I Kings 1:33; II Sam. 13:29.)

N

NILE MONITOR

NILE MONITOR. Familiar to the Children of Israel sojourning in Egypt, the Nile Monitor is a large sand-colored lizard up to 5 or 6 feet in length. Its diet consists largely of smaller lizards, small birds, even tortoises and baby crocodiles that also abound in the Nile.

O

ORYX. The oryx is a species of antelope, distinguished by its extremely long horns. Most common in Arabia it was also found in the Holy Land. Isaiah's animal translated "wild bull" in Isaiah 51:20 might well have referred to the oryx.

ORYX

OYSTER. Though the Jews were forbidden to eat oysters they were familiar with this mollusk because of the pearls found in certain species, plentiful in the adjacent Red Sea and Indian Ocean. Jesus recognized the value of the pearl and used it as an apt symbol of the Kingdom of Heaven in the story of the merchant who, when he found one pearl "of great price, went and sold all that he had, and bought it." (Matt. 13:46.)

OYSTER

OX. The ox, a castrated bull, was an important domestic animal even in pre-biblical times. It was used for plowing, as a draft animal, and was turned loose on the threshing floor where its constant moving about trampled the kernels of grain from the sheath. Jesus was familiar with oxen and must have made many an ox yoke in the carpenter shop at Nazareth, yokes differing little from those used on the oxen of American pioneers. So familiar and important were oxen that Jesus used them as the excuse of the guest refusing the invitation to the banquet: "I have five yoke of oxen and I go to prove them." (Luke 14:19.)

OX

P

PORCUPINE. This comparatively small insect-eating animal was a familiar to the people of Bible days as it is today. It was often found in ruins and in deserted habitations. Curled up into a protective ball, its spines were ample protection against roving dogs or inquisitive man. The porcupine does not "throw" its spines, a mistaken notion held by many people. But they are easily pulled out and their barbed ends make removal a painful process.

An example of the ambiguity of some of the words in the original Hebrew is evident in Isaiah 14:23 which is translated "bittern," a kind of bird. Most scholars now believe the word should be translated "porcupine."

PORCUPINE

R

RAM

RAM. A young ram was often used as a sacrificial animal especially at the Feast of the Passover. Very likely it was of the broadtail species of sheep. The horns of the ram were used as trumpets in battle. We read (Joshua 6:4, 5) that "seven priests bearing trumpets of rams' horns" marched around the walls of Jericho, its walls crumbling on the seventh day after a "long blast." Rams' horns were used to hold liquids, such as oil for anointing. (I Sam. 16:1.)

RAT

RAT. No doubt the rat was as common, and as abhorred, in biblical times as it is today. The word "rat" does not appear in the Bible, but the word **akbar** included all rodents, rats among them. The unsanitary conditions of the times must have made its obnoxious presence inevitable.

The Sand Rat, native to Egypt and eaten by the Arabs, is the Vole, which see.

S

SCORPION

SCORPION. The scorpion has been called "a living fossil" since it is a survivor of the age of the dinosaur. From the many references, from Deuteronomy 8:15 to Revelations 9:3, 10, the scorpion evidently was well known. The most common species in Palestine is the Rock Scorpion. Its body, from 5 to 7 inches long, is made up of eight segments, the last five forming a tail at the end of which is its poisonous stinger. It has eight eyes and four pairs of legs. The pincers in the upper and lower jaws are used to hold its prey while the poison of its sting gradually paralyzes its victim. It lays eggs which hatch in a very short time, the young living on the mother's back.

"If a son . . . shall ask an egg, will he (his father) offer him a scorpion?" (Luke 11:12) is a vivid contrast!

SHARK

SHARK. Sharks have always been found in the Mediterranean and were familiar to the coastal inhabitants of the Holy Land. Strictly speaking, the shark is not a true fish. It is a "selachian," the species of marine life which includes the dogfish and the rays.

The "great fish" in the story of Jonah's adventure could have been a shark. The Great White Shark is capable of swallowing a man, a feat hard to imagine of the whale with its small gullet.

SHEEP. "Abel was a keeper of sheep." (Gen. 4:2.) Thus sheep became the first domesticated animal named in the Bible. And thereafter it is mentioned more than any other animal, 742 times. Thinking perhaps of the shepherd prophet Amos tending his sheep on the hills of Takoha, knowing his sheep and known by them, Jesus referred to himself as "the Good Shepherd." (John 10:14.) Probably the sheep known to Jesus was the fit-tail variety. The tail might weigh as much as 15 pounds. The fat in it is generally considered to be the "fat" mentioned as a sin, guilt or peace offering. (Lev. 3:7, 9; Ex. 29:22; et al.) Young sheep, usually the male (see RAM), were also sacrificed. Familiar with the practice John the Baptist proclaimed Jesus as "the Lamb of God" (John 1:29). The lamb is a well known symbol of our Lord.

SHEEP

SHRIMP. Well known to the Hebrews along the coastal area, this delicious sea creature was forbidden as food since, without fins or scales the Mosaic dietary law classed it as "unclean."

SHRIMP

SNAIL. Snails of many varieties are common throughout the Middle East. Yet outside the mention of it among the "unclean" animals (Lev. 11:30) the only reference is in Psalm 58:8. There the writer speaks of the "snail that melteth away." Among the ancients it was believed that the slimy track left by a crawling snail was substance from its body that in time would be wasted away.

The small marine snail was the source of the important "purple" (actually nearer crimson) dye that colored the robes of Assyrian, Phonecians and Egyptian royalty as early as 1500 B.C.

SNAIL

SNAKE. From the time of Eve's temptation (Gen. 3:1) the serpent, as the snake is usually called in the Bible, has been a common symbol of evil. The Horned Viper, or "Adder," of the Egyptian and Arabian deserts is mentioned 5 times: the reference in Psalm 91:13— "Thou shalt tread upon the young lion and the adder" —is familiar to every Church School pupil. The bite of the adder is extremely poisonous. So, too, is that of the asp, another name for the cobra. Harmless snakes are plentiful throughout the lands of the Bible.

The ancients believed that snakes were immortal, that with each shedding of the skin, life was renewed.

SNAKE

25

SPIDER

SPIDER. The often obnoxious spider is named in Isaiah 30:28 as one of the "four things which are little upon the earth, but . . . are exceeding wise." And one must marvel at the "wisdom" of the spider whose web, a trap for insects upon which the spider feeds, is woven according to a definite pattern of its own species. Even the first small web of the new born spider is an exact minature of that spun by its parents. The web, a liquid exuded by the spider, hardens on contact with the air and is placed in position by the insect's legs—"the spider taketh hold with her hands" is the way it is expressed in Proverbs 30:28.

Not all spiders are weavers but most kinds construct some kind of a web. A few varieties are poisonous.

SPONGE

SPONGE. We are apt to forget that sponges belong to the animal kingdom, even though the lowest form of multicelled creatures. There are many varieties, and since they abound in the waters of the Mediterranean Sea the ancient Hebrews doubtless used them, much as we do today. The mention of the sponge soaked with vinegar and pressed to the lips of Jesus on the cross as a stimulant is mentioned in Matthew, Mark and John.

SWINE. Of all the "unclean" animals the pig seems to have been singled out as the most loathsome. Even the swineherd, tending the pigs, was looked upon with contempt and was barred from the temple. The prodigal son (Luke 15:11ff) sank as low as he could when he tended swine. It was so despised that the strictest of the Jews would not even mention the name. And they believed that they would be polluted if touched by a pig's bristles.

As with the majority of other injunctions against eating certain flesh, the dietary law of the Hebrews was wise. The swine of ancient times were scavangers, their flesh susceptible to hosts that caused various diseases, not the least of which was trichinosis which we guard against today. Moslems are also forbidden to eat pork, no doubt for the same reason.

One might wonder why the herd of swine into which Jesus drove the unclean spirit (Matt. 8:32; Mark 5:13; Luke 8:33) since the Jews were forbidden to raise them. This episode took place in the land of the Gerasenes, a non-Jewish community. The Gerasenes kept and ate swine, as did the Egyptians and the Romans.

SWINE

U

UNICORN. The unicorn, a mythical creature of medieval legend was said to have the head and body of a horse, the hind legs of an antelope, the tail of a lion, the beard of a goat, and a single, long, sharp twisted horn projecting from its head. Actually this imaginary animal had no relation to the real animal the writers of the Bible had in mind. But the English translators of the Jewish scriptures, uncertain as to just what animal was intended in some instances (Num. 23:22; Job 39:9; Psalm 92:10, et al) called it a "unicorn." Later translations have substituted "wild ox" as the likely subject.

URUS. See AUROCH.

UNICORN

URUS

V

VOLE. Water voles, also called "water rats," are found in Europe and much of Asia. The plague of "mice" that beset the Philistines as punishment for the theft of the Ark of the Covenant (I Sam. 6:5) might have been voles. The vole resembles a small muskrat with a short nose, small ears, dark brown in color and about 6 inches long with a 4 inch tail. It builds an underground system of passages, usually near water, hence its name. It feeds on plant roots underground, so destroying the plant or tree.

VOLE

VIPER. There are many kinds of vipers common to the Holy Land, and to much of Europe and Asia. All are poisonous, though some are deadlier than others. "The viper's tongue shall slay him" was the way Job expressed the deadly bite of a viper. Some scholars believe it was the "asp" that Cleopatra permitted to bite her, causing her death.

VIPER

W

WEASEL. Though mentioned by name only in Leviticus 11:29 among the "unclean" animals, the weasel was probably common in the Holy Land. The name of the prophetess consulted by King Josiah when Helkiak found the Book of the Law (I Kings 22:14; II Chron. 34:22) was "Huldah," a name that definitely means "weasel." So the Hebrews were familiar with the animal.

WEASEL

27

WHALE

WHALE. The humpback, the fin whale, and the near relative, the dolphin, are found in the Mediterranean Sea. The Hebrew people living along the seacoast no doubt knew of them, even if seldom seen. The most familiar of the three or four references to the whale in the Bible is the story of Jonah "in the whale's belly." But as mentioned under "Sharks," the words, "a great fish" is the expression used in Jonah 1:17. The Hebrew word translated "whale" is also translated in the Bible as "monster" or "dragon."

WILDCAT

WILDCAT. Although the wildcat is not mentioned by name in the Bible it has always been quite common in the Holy Land. It measures about two feet to the tip of its bushy tail, stands about two feet high at the shoulders, and may weigh up to 15 pounds. Its fur is gray with a black stripe down the middle of the back and across the flanks. Though it occasionally attacks young calves its main fare is birds, mice and other small animals.

WOLF

WOLF. The wolf has always been a beast of prey, in the Holy Land as elsewhere. Protecting his sheep from wolves was one of the shepherd's biggest tasks, especially at night. The wolf with its greed and savagery is referred to some 30 times in the Old Testament. And Jesus warns against "false prophets which come to you in sheep's clothing, but inwardly are ravening wolves." (Matt. 7:15.) And to emphasize the danger that his disciples would encounter he warns, "I send you forth as lambs among wolves." (Luke 10:3.) We can be sure they understood what he meant; he was well acquainted with the wolf and the danger it was to the flocks on the hills about Nazareth.

WORM

WORM. The worm is mentioned many times in the Bible, although almost always the reference is to the maggot or the caterpillar, which see. In an occasional instance, as in Micah 7:17, earthworms are obviously meant: "They . . . shall move out of their holes like worms of the earth." Earthworms have been common everywhere since the world was young.

Z

ZEBU

ZEBU. It is quite possible that the "majesty" (Deut. 33:17) and the "beauty" (Jer. 46:20) rather strangely applied to the ox, were intended for the zebu which it resembles in some respects. The zebu is known as the East Indian ox. It is a much more majestic and noble looking animal than the common ox. With its arched hump, massive shoulders and short horns it was known to the early Persians, Egyptians and Babylonians. A close replica of the zebu is the Brahma bull, now common in parts of this country and used for breeding.

Birds

B

BEARDED VULTURE. See LAMMERGIER.

BEE EATER

BEE EATER. The bee eater, or bee catcher as it is sometimes called, is aptly named since its preferred diet is bees. It is a close relative of the kingfisher, though somewhat smaller. There are several species. The most common is gaily colored with feathers of green, blue and brown. An unusual characteristic, and one which makes the bee eater easily identifiable, is the tail feathers, two of which project noticeably from the middle of the tail.

BITTERN

BITTERN. A shy, solitary bird, and a night prowler, the bittern lives in swampy places where its mottled and striped back of a black and brown color pattern, provide excellent camouflage. Unlike most birds of the heron family, of which it is a member, its neck is short. Nor has it the long wading legs of the heron. The unusually powerful call of the male bittern can be heard a mile away.

Reference to the bittern in Isaiah (14:23) and in Zephaniah (2:14) imply that Babylon and Ninevah were to become as desolate as the swamps in which the bittern lives and sounds its eerie cry.

BLACKBIRD

BLACKBIRD. The blackbird of the Holy Land is a different bird than our wellknown variety. It is nearer brown than black and belongs to the thrush family.

BULBUL

BULBUL. The Hebrews discovered that the bulbul was an easy bird to tame, and with a pleasing song. They kept them in cages outside the doors of their homes, much as we keep canaries and "love birds" today. The bulbul is rather a handsome bird with shiny black feathers. White around the eyes gives it the appearance of wearing spectacles.

C

CHICKEN

CHICKEN. The chicken is a descendant of the Red Jungle Fowl of southern and southwestern Asia. It was domesticated long before the time of the Jewish settlement in the Holy Land. Though the Talmud forbade them from keeping chickens, probably for sanitary reasons lest the flesh of sacrificial animals be contaminated by the insects and larvae that breed in chicken droppings, the regulation was not strictly observed. This is indicated by the familiar words of Jesus: "How often would I have gathered thy children together, even as a hen gathereth her chickens under her wings, and ye would not!" (Matt. 23:34; Luke 13:34).

COCK

COCK. When "cock" is mentioned there comes to mind the picture of the cringing Peter denying his Lord "before the cock crows thrice." (Matt. 26:34.) Most often the cock is mentioned in reference to its habit of crowing an hour or two before dawn. The "cock-crow" was the third watch. Jesus refers to this in Mark 13:35: "Watch ye therefore: for ye know not when the master of the house cometh, at even, or at midnight, or at the cockcrowing, or in the morning." No doubt the crowing of a rooster (cock) was the "alarm clock" of the Israelite farmer then, even as today!

CORMORANT

CORMORANT. Common to the Asian warm countries, the cormorant has two interesting characteristics: though it has webbed feet it often perches on tree branches, and it swims beneath the surface of the water in pursuit of fish. It is nearly 3 feet long, covered with shiny black feathers. Its habit of diving in deep water where it fishes has given it the nickname of "plunger." Today the oriental fishermen train the cormorant to dive and retrieve fish. A ring is first placed around the bird's neck to prevent it from swallowing its catch.

CRANE

CRANE. The crane referred to in Jeremiah 8:7 and again in Isaiah 38:14—"like a crane did I chatter"—was the European variety. The references to its "chatter" was an understatement, perhaps in the translation, as all cranes have powerful voices. They live mostly in swampy areas, subsisting mainly on snakes, insects and small rodents, a fact that makes them useful to the natives and probably fostered the belief that it is considered bad luck to kill a crane. All varieties have long legs and necks.

CROSSBILL. The crossbill is a finch. It lives among evergreens, feeding mostly on conifer seed, its crossed bill being especially adapted for extracting the seed from the cone. It is only about 4 inches in length. The male is a brick red, the female greenish gray. They very much resemble small parrots as they hang from a twig and reach for food.

CROSSBILL

CROW. While the raucous crow we know is not found in the Holy Land, the Carrion Crow of Eurasia and the Hooded Crow no doubt were known. Since these were quite common it may seem strange that the crow is not referred to in the Bible. One logical explanation could be that crow belongs to the raven family and might have been intended in some places where "raven" is used.

CROW

CUCKOO. The cuckoo, spelled "cookow" in all but the late translations of the Bible, was probably the European bird. Feeding mostly on insects, the fact that it does sometimes eat frogs, lizards and small snakes made it "unclean" (Deut. 14:15; Lev. 11:16). It is a very clever imitator of other birds in calls and action. An unusual characteristic of the cuckoo is that some lay blue eggs, others lay buff eggs with black spots. Oftentimes it will lay its eggs in the nest of another bird with eggs of similar colorization, leaving them to be hatched by "foster parents."

D

DOVE. The dove is probably the most familiar bird in the Bible, first mentioned when it was sent out by Noah, returning to the ark with an olive branch in its beak as evidence that it had found land. (Gen. 8:11.) There are many varieties of doves in the Holy Land, the Rock Dove or Pigeon (which see) and the Turtle Dove the most common. They are monagamous, both male and female helping to build the nest, incubate the eggs and care for the young. The newly hatched birds are nourished with "pigeon's milk, a substance secreted by the wall of the bird's stomach and regurgitated. Doves are characteristically gently and often used as symbols of beauty and loveliness, as in the Song of Solomon.

CUCKOO

All four gospels speak of the Spirit of God descending "like a dove" when Jesus was baptised. Hence the dove has become the symbol of the third member of the Trinity.

DOVE

DUCK

DUCK. Though not mentioned in the Bible, we can be sure that ducks were well known to the Israelites. Like the goose they doubtless were served at King Solomon's banquets and in the humblest Hebrew home. There is no record that they were domesticated. Wild ducks are still plentiful in Palestine.

E

EAGLE. Some species of eagle is found in almost every part of the world. The Holy Land is no exception. Of the three or four kinds found there, the Golden Eagle is probably the one most often referred to in the Bible. It is dark brown, the back of its neck tinged with gold feathers, hence its name. It has a wingspread of 6 feet or more.

EAGLE

The swiftness of the eagle's flight, its keen eyesight and its longevity are used as illustrations throughout the Bible to illustrate a parable (Ezek. 17:3-10); to emphasize a situation (Deut. 29:49); to teach a lesson (Jer. 49:16). And there is something exalting in the declaration of Isaiah (40:31) that "they that wait upon the Lord . . . shall mount up with wings as eagles." In some instances Bible references to the "vulture" may have been translated "eagle." Both are of the same family and quite similar when airborne.

F

FALCON. Several varieties of the falcon, a branch of the hawk family, are found in the Holy Land. In most species the male is smaller than the female. Usually a pair remain mated for life. Both help build the nest, incubate the eggs and raise the young.

FALCON

The Peregrine Falcon has been used for hunting since ancient times; falconry was a common sport in medieval England. But there is no record that the Hebrews used them in this way.

FINCH. Of the many varieties of finch, several are found in Palestine. Both the Trumpeter Bullfinch with its distinctive piping note, and the brightly colored Goldfinch were kept as caged pets in Jesus' time, as they are today in many parts of Asia. Because of its habit of eating thistles and thorns the goldfinch became the symbol of Christ's Crown of Thorns and so of the Passion of Christ.

FINCH

FLAMINGO. The long-legged, long-necked flamingo was one of the many wading birds abundant in the Nile delta close to the site of the Israelites sojourn in Egypt. They must have been familiar to the Hebrews then, and later in Palestine when flocks of water birds, including the flamingo, inhabited the swamps around the Sea of Galilee.

FLAMINGO

FOWL. We think of a hen as a fowl, and this has come to be the common meaning of the word. But "fowl" in the Bible had little if any reference to adult chickens. Rather the word is used in a general sense to include all birds: God gave man "dominion over the fowl of the air." (Gen. 1:26.) When Jesus bids his listeners to "behold the fowls of the air" that "neither toil nor spin" (Matt. 6:26) he obviously was not thinking of barnyard fowl, i.e. the hen.

FOWL

G

GOOSE. Though not mentioned by name in the Bible, carvings on the walls of ancient Egyptian tombs indicate that geese were known as early as 2500 B.C. The captive Children of Israel surely knew them. It is quite likely that the "fatted fowl," a part of Solomon's provisions for one day (I Kings 23:4) were geese, possibly the Red-breasted Goose, still seen in Egypt and in parts of the Holy Land.

GOOSE

GRIFFON. A species of vulture, the griffon glides gracefully high in the air, swooping down to earth with amazing speed and precision when its keen eyesight locates a meal, usually a dead animal, far below. Then it may gorge itself until it is unable to fly. It is light brown, its neck and head nearly bare, covered only with fine down. The Egyptians and the Persians used the griffon as an emblem of royal power.

GRIFFON

GULL. An occasional sea-gull doubtless "wandered" inland as far as the Sea of Galilee, acquainting the natives with the bird. And to those Israelites who lived near the coast of the Mediterranean Sea, and to Peter and the apostles who came to Joppa on the coast (Acts 9:36), soaring, screaming sea-gulls were a familiar sight.

GULL

HAWK

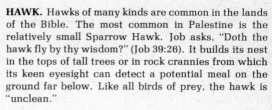

HAWK. Hawks of many kinds are common in the lands of the Bible. The most common in Palestine is the relatively small Sparrow Hawk. Job asks, "Doth the hawk fly by thy wisdom?" (Job 39:26). It builds its nest in the tops of tall trees or in rock crannies from which its keen eyesight can detect a potential meal on the ground far below. Like all birds of prey, the hawk is "unclean."

HERON. Herons are characterized by their long legs, long neck and long, pointed beak. The blue-gray heron is common in the Holy Land where it winters. It builds its nest in swamps and along river banks, often in a tall tree, returning to the same nest year after year. Quite often many nests are close together forming a colony. Although some kinds of heron might be classed as "unclean" under the Mosaic dietary law, all are on the forbidden list.

HERON

The Great White Heron is found in the swamps of Syria. Common, too, is the black-crowned Night Heron with a thicker beak and shorter legs than most of the heron family.

HOOPOE. The hoopoe is an attractive bird, especially with its crest of reddish feathers erected and expanded when it is alarmed. It is a fairly large bird, about 10 inches long, salmon-pink with zebra-like stripes on its back, wings and tail. The nesting and feeding habits of the hoopoe do not match the attractive appearance of the bird. It does nothing to keep its nest in repair once it is built. During the incubation period an oil gland at the base of the female's tail exudes an intensely unpleasant fluid to discourage would-be invaders. This, along with the fact that it has a habit of probing into filth for worms and insects gave the Hebrews sufficient reason for classing it as "unclean."

HOOPOE

I

IBIS

IBIS. The Ibis, sacred to Thoth, Egyptian god of learning, was common among the tall Papyrus in which the baby Moses was hidden. Now it is seldom seen along the lower Nile. Over 2 feet from its slender arched bill to its tail feathers, with the long, thin legs of the wading birds, it was well known to the Children of Israel before the exodus.

K

KESTREL. The Kestrel is one of the smaller falcons, and is still found in Palestine. Like all falcons, it is an excellent flyer, but a unique characteristic of the kestrel is its ability to hover in mid-air, its long, pointed wings extended. This has given it the name of "wind hover." It feeds mostly on small rodents and insects. Kestrels are often seen in flocks of twenty or more.

KESTREL

KITE. A migratory bird, the Kite summers along the Dead Sea and in the mountains of southern Judea. Like the falcon, it is a member of the hawk family. It is the greatest scavanger of the family, feeding on carrion, which assures it a place among the "unclean." But it is a magnificent bird with a long, forked tail and chestnut plumage. Like all hawks, its flight is graceful and buoyant.

KITE

L

LAMMERGIER. This is the "ossifrage" mentioned in Deuteronomy 14:12. It is a species of vulture and the largest of the species with a wing spread of up to 9 feet. It has been called the most magnificent of the birds of prey. Like most of the vulture family it nests on cliffs. It feeds largely on the marrow inside the bones that other vultures have picked clean. To get at the marrow it carries the bones high in the air, then lets them drop upon the rocks to shatter the bone.

Because of the tassels of feathers that hang from its beak it is sometimes called the Bearded Vulture.

LAMMERGIER

LAPWING. The Lapwing of Eurasia is a colorful bird, its dark green irridescent feathers splashed with brown above and white below, and with a black chest band. A curving crest decorates the back of the neck. About a foot long, it has stubby wings and the long legs typical of the plover family to which it belongs. But unlike the plover it is not a shore bird and is usually found inland. Its eggs were once considered a real delicacy.

LAPWING

O

OSSIFRAGE. See LAMMERGIER.

OSSIFRAGE

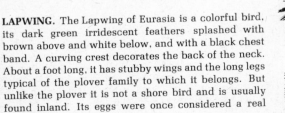

OSPREY

OSTRICH

OWL, SCOOPS

OWL, EAGLE

PARTRIDGE

OSPREY. Spelled "ospray" in O. T. (Lev. 11:13; Deut. 14:12) this is a large fish hawk. Its head, neck and under parts are white, the back and wings a dark brown with a blackish cast. Soaring high over the water its keen eyes sight a fish. With wings folded it dives. It strikes the water feet first, often disappearing beneath the surface for a moment, emerging with a fish clutched in its talons. Then spreading its broad wings it flies off to enjoy its catch. After which it returns to fly low over the water to wash its feet.

OSTRICH. The ostrich, up to 8 feet in height, is the largest bird in the world. It once existed as far north as Syria and so was known to the early Hebrews. Job has much to say about the ostrich, none of it very complimentary. (Job 39:13-18.) And it is true that the bird is not known for its intelligence—but it does **not** hide its head in the sand when danger threatens! It can run as fast as 40 miles an hour and so can outrun most danger, but if forced to fight it can deal terrific blows with its hoof-like toes. It cannot fly. Its cry, likened to the bellowing of a suffering bull, probably is what Micah had in mind when he speaks of "mourning like the ostriches." (Mich. 1:8.) "Owls" is used in the King James version, but "ostriches" are doubtless what the prohpet meant.

OWL. In listing the unclean birds in Leviticus 11:17 the writer mentions "the little owl" and "the great owl." This is not strange since there are many species of owls in the Holy Land. Very likely "little owl" referred to the "Scoops Owl," only about 8 inches long. The large Eagle Owl might well be the "great owl" with a body up to 2 feet in length, strong claws and cruel beak. Owls are nocturnal creatures, spending their daylight hours in ruins and caves. (Isaiah 13:21; Jer. 50:39.)

The owl is the only bird whose eyes are turned forward and cannot be turned in their sockets. In order to see to either side it must turn its head. Its sight and hearing are both very keen.

P

PARTRIDGE. The partridge is widely distributed throughout the northern hemisphere. There are several kinds in the Holy Land. The most common is the "Chuker." It is covered with brightly colored feathers. The Sand Partridge is less colorful, its buff and brown plumage making it less conspicuous in the wilderness area of Judea. All varieties are hunted for food. Though a fast runner it tires quickly. Hunters pursue it on horseback until the bird is exhausted when it may be caught with the bare hands. Perhaps this is what David had in mind when he says that Saul came after him "as when one doth hunt a partridge in the mountains." (I Sam. 26:20.)

PEACOCK. The pomp and glitter of King Solomon's court was greatly enhanced by the gorgeous peacocks brought from India and the tropics by the navy of Hiram, king of Tyre. (I Kings 10:22; II Chron. 9:21.) They then spread to other countries in the Mediterranean areas.

PEACOCK

The peacock, the male peafowl, with its gleaming colored breast and outspread tail of dazzling colors, has been called the most beautiful bird in the world. It became a symbol of immortality to the early Christians, probably because of the legendary belief that peacock flesh does not decay.

PELICAN. The pelican is one of the most curious looking of birds. The long, flattened beak with a large pouch under the lower mandible, its small head, short legs and massive body give it a somewhat ludicrous appearance as it awkwardly waddles along on land. But in the air it glides with grace on a wingspan of up to 8 feet. Suddenly it dives straight down, landing with a splash and spearing the fish it has sighted.

PELICAN

The pelican's method of feeding its young is peculiar. The mother opens its beak wide and the young pluck food from the mother's crop. This strange procedure led the ancients to believe that the pelican fed its young with its own blood. Thus the pelican became the symbol of mercy in ancient art, perhaps emphasized by the words of the psalmist: "I am like a pelican in the wilderness" (Psalm 122:6) (seeking God's mercy).

PHARAOH'S HEN. This is a small vulture, common in Egypt as the name would imply. But it is also abundant on the plains of Sharon and the hills to the south, especially in the Kedron valley. It is white with black wings. Its large nest is built of sticks, rubbish and even old rags. It wanders about the village streets eating garbage and refuse that other vultures will not touch.

PHARAOH'S HEN

PHOENIX. Ancient legend gave the phoenix to Christianity as a symbol of the resurrection. It was a mythical bird, said to be very beautiful, quite large, and living 500 years or more. Then it set its nest on fire and was consumed in the flames, only to rise from the ashes to begin a new life cycle. Some scholars believe that Job was referring to this fantastic creature in the word translated "sand" in Job 29:18. The phoenix is not among the birds mentioned by Job, nor is it mentioned elsewhere in the Bible.

PHOENIX

PIGEON

PIGEON. The rock dove of Eurasia is closely related to the turtle dove (which see) but it is a different branch of the family. It has been bred for 5,000 years and the breeding of pigeons is a popular hobby today. The ability of the homing pigeon to find its way back to its loft from a great distance is one of nature's so far unfathomed mysteries.

Q

QUAIL. The quail mentioned in the Bible (Ex. 16:11-13; Num. 11:31, 32; Psalm 105:40, etc.) is not much larger than a robin. Its feathers are brown and black except for those on the belly which are white. Small as it is the quail is still hunted for food as it was long before the Hebrew immigration to the Holy Land. The deluge of quail mentioned in Numbers 11 . . . "two cubits high on the face of the earth" — no doubt is an exaggeration. But during the fall migration great numbers of them cloud the sky. Unlike other birds, the quail do not migrate en masse. Instead, the migration may be spread over a month or two. Not a particularly good flyer, it covers the migratory route in short distances, often settling on the ground overnight. And often so exhausted that they can be caught with bare hands. Nets are sometimes used to capture them.

QUAIL

R

RAVEN. The raven is the first bird mentioned in the Bible: "At the end of forty days . . . Noah . . . sent forth a raven" (Gen. 8:7) to see if the waters had receded. Male and female, who pair for life, share in incubating and in feeding the young birds. However, the raven's unsavory reputation is deserved. It attacks smaller, weaker creatures, often pecking out their eyes. They are predatory by nature, feeding on carrion.

In spite of their deserved reputation and uncouth habits, ravens are intelligent birds and can be trained to talk, parrot fashion. The raven with its "Nevermore" in Edgar Allen Poe's poem is not poetic fancy!

RAVEN

S

SPARROW. In picking a bird to represent the humblest of creatures, Jesus chose the sparrow: "Are not two sparrows sold for a farthing? And one of them shall not fall to the ground without your Father (knowing)" (Matt. 10:29). Sparrows are gregarious birds, flocks of them as common in Bible times as today. The psalmist might well have had this fact in mind when, alone and desolate, he write, "I am as a sparrow alone upon a house top." (Psalm 102:7.) Though there are instances in the Old Testament where "sparrow" might mean any small bird, there is no doubt that many varieties were as familiar to the ancient Hebrews as to us.

SPARROW

STORK. One of man's favorite birds, the stork's purported association with human childbirth is common the world over. This may have come about originally because of the stork's loyalty to its young, both parents assisting in their incubation and care. The Hebrew word for "stork" means "kindly one" or "loyal one," both titles which one likes to think of as applying to human parents.

The stork is mute; it has no voice box. It communicates by rapidly clapping its bill or through movements of its head, neck and beak. Feeding on frogs, fish, rodents and lizards as well as insect, it is on the "unclean" list.

STORK

SWALLOW. The swift and graceful flight of the swallow as it darts through the air catching insects, was well known to the Israelites. Its habit of building its nest in barns, and even houses, might well have prompted the psalmist to write, "Yea, the sparrow hath found a house, and the swallow a nest for herself where she may lay her young, even thine altars, O Lord of Hosts." (Psalm 84:3.)

The swallow, sometimes called "martin," was very likely confused with the swift by the early writers of the Bible (See SWIFT). They are very similar in appearance, but not related.

SWALLOW

SWAN. Though the swan, common in Egypt, must have been known to the Children of Israel, there is no mention of this graceful long-necked water-bird in the Bible except in the list of "unclean" birds. (Lev. 11:13, 18.)

SWAN

SWIFT. Often confused with the swallow because of its similar appearance and behavior, the swift is a member of the humming bird family. It is probably the fastest of flyers with much of its life spent in the air. Its legs are so short that its take-off from the ground is slow. When it alights for the night it clings to a crack or crevice in a cliff, in position for immediate flight.

SWIFT

V

VULTURE. (See GRIFFON; LAMMERGIER). One of the most detested of scavengers, the vulture plays a most important part in nature's plan, feeding on and so disposing of carrion. This fact was well known to the Israelites and there are many places in the Old Testament in which the vulture is plainly indicated by references to "fowls of the air" that eat dead flesh. (I Kings 14:11; Psalm 79:2; Prov. 30:17, etc.)

VULTURE

Plants

A

ACACIA

ACACIA. The acacia is native to Egypt and so was known to the early Hebrews who called it the "shittah tree." (Isa. 41:19.) On their exodus from Egypt they carried with them wood of this tree and used it in building the Ark of the Covenant. (Ex. 25:10.) Considered sacred, it was never used for other than religious purposes. Some scholars think its spiny growth might have been used to make Jesus' crown of thorns.

ACORUS

ACORUS. Oil pressed from the roots of the acorus was used for anointing. It is a rushlike plant, native to the eastern Mediterranean region. Leaves of the plant were sometimes strewn on the floors of places of worship in place of carpeting.

ALMOND

ALMOND. Only the olive and the fig are more commonly cultivated in the Holy Land than the almond. The pink or white blossoms cover the branches before the leaves appear as early as January. They resemble our peach blossoms which is not strange since botanically the almond is a member of the peach family. While the nut is universally popular and delicious eating, it is also crushed to produce almond oil, widely used for flavoring and in cosmetics. Wild almonds grow in some sections of Palestine.

ALOES (O.T.). There are two "aloes" referred to in the Bible, differing widely. The "lign aloes" of Numbers 24:6, also called "eaglewood," is a large spreading tree with leaves resembling those of the peach. The inner wood is soft and fragrant leading the psalmist to write, "All thy garments smell of myrrh and aloes." (Psalm 45:8.)

ALOES O.T.

ALOES (N.T.). Entirely different than the aloes above is the aloes mixed with myrrh that Nicodemus and Joseph of Arimathea used in preparing the body of Jesus for burial. (John 19:38-40.) This aloes is a succulent plant with large spikelike leaves and bearing bell shaped reddish yellow flowers. It is common in the warmer sections of this country. The crushed leaves yield a sap quite commonly used in medicinal lotions.

ALOES N.T.

ANEMONE. Sometimes called the "windflower," the anemone is related to the buttercup. It grows profusely in Palestine. In early spring its vividly colored flowers carpet the plains with acres of color, ranging from white to purple, with the red anemone especially striking. It is believed by many scholars that these were the "lilies of the field" to which Jesus was referring when he told his listeners that "Solomon in all his glory was not arrayed like one of these." (Luke 12:27.)

ANEMONE

ANISE (DILL). When Jesus berated the scribes and Pharisees for confining their holiness to the tithing of "mint and anise" (Matt. 23:23) the reference was most likely to the common dill since anise was rare in the Holy Land. But the tall feathery plants of dill with their clusters of small yellow flowers and abundant seed were found everywhere. Even as today, it was used as a spice and for flavoring.

ANISE

APRICOT. The apricot is one of the most abundant fruits in Palestine. It grows profusely on the highlands and in the lowlands around the Jordan. Since the apple is comparitively recent, the forbidden fruit growing in the Garden of Eden may well have been the apricot. The Hebrew word translated "apple" in the Song of Solomon 2:3 and the fruit mentioned in Joel 1:12 could have been the Golden Apricot.

APRICOT

ASPALATHUS. This is a thorny shrub, growing from four to five feet high with narrow leaves along the stem. The very fragrant white and pink blossoms are shaped somewhat like the Morning Glory. From it was derived ointment and perfume. The writer of Ecclesiasticus (24:15) refers to it: "I gave a sweet smell like cinnamon and aspalathus."

ASPALATHUS

ASTRAGAL. This spiny dwarf shrub yields the "gum tragacanth" of commerce. It has pale yellow pea-like flowers and long, needle-sharp thorns that point in all directions. There are many varieties, some found on the shores of the Dead Sea, others growing high up on the summit of Mount Hermon.

ASTRAGAL

B

BALSAM

BARLEY

BAY TREE

BDELLIUM

BEAN

BALSAM. A low-growing tree, the balsam is native to southern Arabia. It is said that the Queen of Sheba brought seeds to King Solomon who had groves of balsam planted so that the fragrant and medicinal "balm" made from the sap of the tree might be available. The "balm of Gilead," mentioned several times in the Old Testament (Jer. 8:22; Ezek. 27:17, etc.) is believed by many to be this product of the balsam.

BARLEY. Barley was a common grain when the Israelites were in Egypt. During one of the plagues that beset the land "the barley was smitten." (Ex. 9:31.) It became important in Palestine and is still grown extensively. It is sown in late fall and gathered in the spring. Then a second sowing is made. It was five barley loaves, along with two small fishes that the lad in John 6:9 gave to Jesus with which to feed the multitude.

BAY TREE. David's reference to the "green bay tree" (Psalm 37:35) as a symbol of the spreading power of the wicked is an apt illustration. Actually the "spreading" is from the many shoots that sprout near the main stem. It is the "laurel" later used by Rome for the crown awarded the victors in sports and in war.

BDELLIUM. According to Genesis 2:12 bdellium was planted in the Garden of Eden. It is an ancient tree having small, inconspicuous blossoms and long thorns. From it comes a fragrant gum which, hardening on exposure to the air, forms almost transparent globules with a whitish tinge. Hence the reference in Numbers 11:7, "the manna was as corriander seed, and the colour thereof as the color of bdellium."

BEAN. The bean is an ancient vegetable and has long been a staple article of diet in the Middle East. The bean referred to in II Samuel 17:28 was not unlike the bush bean known to present day gardeners; though more robust, sometimes growing to a height of two or three feet. The familiar pea-shaped blossoms are white with a black spot on some of the petals. And scented.

Our present system of voting with white and black balls originated in ancient times when beans were used. Then, as now, white showed approval, black signified a "no" vote.

42

BETHLEHEM STAR. Though its half dozen elongated yellow petals forming a "star" appear fragile, the Bethlehem Star is a hardy plant. It favors northern exposures and grows in damp, stony ground, blossoming in early winter.

This plant is not to be confused with the Star of Bethlehem, which see.

BETHLEHEM STAR

BRAMBLE. The Palestian bramble (Judges 9:14) is similar to our common blackberry. It is just as strong a grower with equally numerous sharp thorns. The blossoms have a pinkish tinge. The delicious berries are a deep purple.

BRAMBLE

BULRUSH. It was easy to conceal the child Moses among the bulrushes for they grew thickly along the banks of the Mile to a height of twelve feet or more. The individual stalks are very pliable, easily made into "an ark" to hold the baby. (Ex. 2:3.) The blossoms at the top of the long reed resemble a plume of wispy feathers.

BULRUSH

C

CAMPHIRE. When King Solomon writes, "My beloved is unto me as a cluster of camphire in the vineyards" (Song of Sol. 1:14) we can be sure that the camphire is a delightful plant. It is shrub-like plant, about ten feet high with very fragrant creamy-white blossoms that grow in clusters. The camphire is the "henna" from which comes the rusty-red commercial dye of that name.

CAMPHIRE

CAMPION. Also called Egyptian Pink or Catchfly, the campion is one of the most common varieties of pinks found in Palestine. Only about 6 inches high, it grows abundantly around the Sea of Galilee, its blossoming in early February marking the beginning of spring.

CAMPION

CALYCOTOME

CALYCOTOME. The golden color of the calycotome, a gray, prickly shrub, welcomes spring in most regions of the Holy Land. The fragrant yellow blossoms resemble small orchids. The hairy seed pods, much like pea pods, begin to ripen as soon as the petals fall, the ripening continuing through the dry summer months. Though used extensively for fencing and for fuel the calycotome is always plentiful, spreading rapidly in dry soil where little other vegetation can survive.

CAPER

CAPER. This small inconspicuous plant with flowers of white, having rose-magenta filaments with yellow tips, trails over the rocky cliffs so profusely as to cover the ground with its dark green leaves. Thorns grow along the stem. In the familiar passage of Ecclesiastes 12:5 we read, "the grasshopper shall be a burden, and **desire** shall fail." The original Hebrew reads, "the **caper** shall fail" (to grow?).

CAROB TREE

CAROB TREE. While not mentioned by name in the Bible, the carob tree was familiar to the Hebrew people since it is native to the lands of the eastern Mediterranean area. An evergreen, it grows up to 50 feet in height. It bears large think pods used for food for swine and cattle, and even for people. The "husks" which the swine and the prodigal son ate were very likely these pods which are called "locusts." In the East they are known as "John's bread" and accepted as the "locusts" eaten by John the Baptist. (Matt. 3:4.)

CASSIA

CASSIA. Cassia was one of the "principal spices" which the Lord bade Moses use in preparing "an oil of holy anointment" with which to anoint the tabernacle. (Ex. 30:24f.) The spice is made from the bark of the tree. The buds are often used in place of cloves. A purgative is made from the young leaves and seed pods.

44

CEDAR. One of the best known trees of the Holy Land is the cedar, of which there are several kinds. It is referred to often in the Bible, and naturally so since it was used for many purposes, from musical instruments to timbers for Solomon's palace.

A smaller cedar is native to the plains of Galilee. It grows only about 20 feet high with glistening foliage and brown berries instead of cones. This cedar is believed to be the cedar burned in the sacrificial ritual at the temple altar. (Num. 19:6.)

The "cedars of Lebanon are mentioned several times in the Old Testament. Twelve of the oldest and largest are still standing, revered by Christians, Jews and Mohammedons.

CEDAR

CHRYSANTHEMUM. There is little resemblance between the cultivated chrysanthemum with which we are familiar and the Garland Chrysanthemum of Palestine. The yellow flower, blossoming along the top of the two foot stem, looks more like a daisy with widespread petals, or a small sunflower. It blooms in March.

CHRYSANTHEMUM

CISTUS. The large lavender-pink cistus is a spring flower. It has commercial value since ladanum, a fragrant gum, is derived from the plant. Some scholars believe that the "myrrh" referred to in Genesis 43:11 was from the cistus.

CISTUS

CLEMATIS. This is also known as Buckthorn. Growing in dry, unfertile areas where only a few plants survive, the clematis seems to prepare for a grand exhibit when the rainy season comes. Then the hills are covered with its green tinted creamy-white blossoms. Though a shrub, a fully grown plant is almost tree size. The flowers grow at the end of short branches, hanging downward. The bark of the clematis has a sweet taste of which ants are very fond.

CLEMATIS

COCKLE. "Let cockle (grow) instead of barley" (Job 31:40) was Job's way of insisting on his integrity, inviting punishment if he were guilty of wrong doing. Though a rather beautiful plant, some four feet high with veined pink flowers on its spreading stalks, it is a noxious weed. The seeds are poisonous if used as flour.

COCKLE

45

CORN

CORN. "Corn" in the Bible refers to almost all kinds of grain, as it does today in many countries. Our corn was unknown to the people of the Bible.

CORNFLOWER. The Palestinian Cornflower is much the same as our familiar "Bachelor Button." It is a deep blue, growing profusely over the hills of much of the Middle East.

CORNFLOWER

CORIANDER. The coriander grows wild in Palestine and was known as early as 1550 B.C. It belongs to the carrot family but the plants grow to a height of two feet. The leaves resemble parsley. The small white or pinkish blossoms grow in clusters at the end of the flower stem. The seeds are the important part of the plant. They are pressed for the oil they yield, this being used for both culinary and medicinal purposes.

CORIANDER

COTTON. Cotton is not mentioned by name in the King James version of the Bible, but the later versions describe the hangings in the king's palace as "white cotton curtains." (Esther 1:6.) Cotton was grown in Egypt for centuries before the Christian era and was cultivated by the Jews after their settlement in the Holy Land. It was processed much as it was in this country before the advent of the cotton gin.

COTTON

CRADLEWORT. This is also called "Our Lady's Bedstraw," legend saying that cradlewort filled the manger in which Mary placed the Christ child. Some of the paintings of the old masters show cradlewort in pictures of the Nativity. It is a fragile plant, covered with puffs of small, sweet-scented yellow flowers.

CRADLEWORT

CROCUS. This harbinger of spring, blossoming before the snow has gone, was familiar to the people of the Bible. One form is native to the Mediterranean area and no doubt was as eagerly looked for as a sign of spring as it is today.

CROCUS

CROWFOOT. The small glossy yellow blossoms of the crowfoot (often called Jerusalem Crowfoot) resembles the familiar buttercup. The finely divided foliage has a grayish tinge. It grows profusely in the rocky soil of Palestine.

CROWFOOT

CROWN IMPERIAL. Borne at the end of a stiff, upright stem are the drooping flower-cups of the Crown Imperial. These are red and yellow. Legend says they were once white, lifted up and blooming in the Garden of Gethsemane. The night Jesus sought the peace of the garden, all the flowers bowed their heads except the proud Crown Imperial. At the rebuke of Jesus they hung their heads and red and yellow took the place of the white of innocence.

CROWN IMPERIAL

CUMMIN. Cummin has been cultivated since ancient times. It is a small, rather fragile plant about 12 inches in height with umbels of dainty pink and white flowers. It is cultivated for the seeds which are crushed and used for flavoring and for medicinal purposes. It was valuable enough to be part of the required tithe, but not to be compared with the "weightier matters of the law." (Matt. 23:23.)

CUMMIN

CYCLAMEN. Growing abundantly throughout much of the Middle East, the cyclamen is called "Cock of the Mountains" by the Arabs. It has been dedicated to Mary because the "red throat" at the heart of the flower looks like a drop of blood, symbolizing the sword of sorrow that pierced Mary's heart when her Son was crucified. It has been described as "a strange flower with bent back, curved petals, and crimson eye looking down as if expectant of the earth to yield treasure to it."

CYCLAMEN

CYPRESS

CYPRESS. This is the "gopher wood" referred to in Genesis 6:14, used to build the ark. It was once common on the mountains of Palestine. Because of its great durability it was extensively used for building ships. Gradually the supply was depleted. Since "cypress" and "cedar" are both translations of the same Hebrew word we cannot always be certain which was intended.

D

DAISY

DAISY. Although it does not grow as high as our daisy, nor is it as robust, the daisy of the Holy Land bears a close resemblance otherwise. Its petals are often edged with pink. It is especially abundant in moist areas of the hills, blooming in October and continuing to bloom until the following summer.

DANDELION. Lands bordering the Mediterranean were the original home of the dandelion. From there it spread around the world. In ancient times, as now, the leaves were used in salads. Quite likely it is one of the "bitter herbs" often mentioned in the Bible: the bitter taste of older dandelion leaves is familiar to us.

DANDELION

DATE PALM. It is thought that the Date Palm may be the oldest known species of tree cultivated by man. After the exodus from Egypt the Hebrew people took the date palm as a sacred emblem, perhaps because of its importance as a source of food. Also because date palms growing in the desert was an indication of life-giving water in the area. It is the main food supply for man and beast in the desert regions today as it has been for countless centuries. The palm—there are several varieties—is referred to more than sixty times in the Bible, from Judges 4:5 when we read that "Deborah dwelt under the palm tree" to the waving of palm branches on the first Palm Sunday.

DATE PALM

F

FIG. Ranking with the date palm as one of the most valuable trees of ancient times is the Fig. Its pear-shaped fruit was important as food. To the Hebrews this beautiful spreading tree was a symbol of abundance and peace. It is mentioned in Genesis 3:7 as growing in the Garden of Eden and Jesus refers to the fig and the fig tree several times. To the Egyptians it represented the Tree of Life. Its importance to the life and commerce of peoples in the Middle East is still great.

FIG

FIR. The fir of the Holy Land is a variety of pine, common in the area west of the Jordan. It is similar to our pines, having silver-gray bark and reddish-brown cones that take on a grayish tinge when fully opened. The needles grow in pairs.

Hiram, king of Tyre, "gave Solomon . . . fir trees" (I Kings 5:10) to be used in the building of the temple. Tyrpentine and resin were by-products of the fir in ancient times.

FIR

FLAG. In Exodus 2:3, 5 the flag is mentioned in connection with the hiding of the baby Moses. It was one of the many rank growing plants that thrive in wet ground. It is natural that they be mentioned along with the bulrushes. As Job asks, "Can the flag grow without water?" (Job 8:11).

Entirely different from the swampland flag mentioned above is the Corn Flag indigenous to Palestine. It grows mostly in the grainfields, its deep pink blossoms changing to purple as they grow older, coloring the fields before the grain ripens in early April.

FLAG

FLAX. The oldest textile fibre in the world is that of flax. From it linen has been made for thousands of years. Probably "linen" is meant in Hosea 2:5, 9 when the prophet mentions "wool and flax." The common flax has a yellowish stem with bright blue flowers. The pink flax is also abundant in the Holy Land, blossoming in late March or early April.

FLAX

FRANKINCENSE. The frankincense tree, source of the spice which the magi brought to Bethlehem (Matt. 2:10), resembles our Mountain Ash. It is a rather large tree with star-shaped pink flowers having yellow centers. The resin, from which comes the incense and the spice, is obtained by making incisions in the bark of the tree. As the sap flows out it hardens and becomes brittle. It burns freely, giving off the fragrance for which it is known. Once plentiful in the Near East it has become increasingly scarce.

FRANKINCENSE

G

GALBANUM. The galbanum plant resembles anise (dill). A perennial, it grows several feet in height. It has finely divided leaves and umbels of small greenish-white blossoms. As indicated in Exodus 30:34, it was one of the "sweet spices" to be used in the preparation of sacred ointment.

GALBANUM

GALL. See POPPY.

GERANIUM

GERANIUM. We think of the geranium as a cultivated bedding plant in our gardens, growing the year around where winters are warm. In the lands of the Bible it grows wild on the hillsides and in the valleys. It closely resembles our popular member of the family.

GLADIOLI

GLADIOLI. Called "Sword Lily" in Palestine, the native gladiolus derives its name from the curved petals that resemble an eastern scimitar. The blossoms, smaller than our cultivated variety, are pink or purple and grow along one side of the short stem.

GRAPE

GRAPE. Grapes and vineyards are mentioned early and often in the Bible, from Genesis 9:20 to Revelation 14:18, sometimes literally (Deut. 23:24), often as metaphor (Hosea 9:10). While the grapes themselves were of greatest importance as food and for making wine, the beauty of the vineyards in blossom could not have escaped attention. Except that the harvest began in June, vineculture was much the same in Bible times as now.

H

HEMLOCK

HEMLOCK. The hemlock that "springeth . . . in the furrows of the field" (Hosea 10:4) is a poisonous plant, some 5 feet in height with dark fern-like leaves. It has small white blossoms in umbels on branching stems. Both seed and plant when crushed yield a poisonous substance which can be fatal when taken internally. This was the hemlock which Socrates drank.

HUMBUM. The Arabs named this plant which decorates the rocky areas of Palestine and neighboring countries. The blossoms, ranging in color from white to blue, cover the tall stalks. The flowers resemble forget-me-nots. The plant has a practical use as the leaves are used as poultices. And also as food.

HUMBUM

HYACINTH. The blue, bell-shaped flowers of the hyacinth bloom profusely throughout the Holy Land in February and March. They are especially abundant on Mt. Carmel and near Sidon. The smaller Grape Hyacinth is also found throughout Palestine.

HYACINTH

HYSSOP. There are two "hyssops" referred to in the Bible. In the Old Testament David prays, "Purge me with hyssop and I shall be clean." (Ps. 51:7.) The reference here, as in other places in the Old Testament, is an herblike plant belonging to the mint family. It has a pungent taste and a spicy odor. In some Jewish religious rites it was sprinkled over the sacrifice as a symbolic purifying agent.

HYSSOP O.T.

The hyssop mentioned in the New Testament is a member of the sorghum family. It is sometimes called "Jerusalem Corn." The large seed heads, ground into meal, constitute the main part of the diet for many people in the Near East. Some scholars believe that this was the "parched corn" that Boaz gave to Ruth. (Ruth 2:14.)

The strong stems of the plant grow to a height of 6 feet or more. Which indicates how **this** hyssop was used at Calvary when "they filled a sponge with vinegar, and put it **upon** hyssop, and put it to his mouth." (John 19:29.)

HYSSOP N.T.

J

JUNIPER. The "juniper" mentioned by Job (Job 30:4) and in Psalm 120:4, is an incorrect translation of the Hebrew name for one of the most common flowering shrubs in all Judea. It actually is the "Flowering Broom," a member of the pea family with pealike clusters of delicate pale pink or white blossoms, followed by pods containing two rows of small, bitter pealike seeds. It is used extensively as fuel. And although the leaves are small the plant furnishes a measure of welcome shade in the desert, as when Elijah "came down and sat under a juniper tree." (I Kings 19:4.)

JUNIPER

L

LENTIL

LENTIL. The lentil, from which Jacob made the pottage for his weary brother Esau (Gen. 26:29ff) is a pealike plant resembling vetch. The trailing vine grows in soil too poor for other plants. It is common in most of the Middle East, and in Egypt.

LILY

LILY. The lily, in many varieties, has been growing in the Holy Land since time immemorial. As far back as 3000 B.C. it was a sacred emblem in Crete. Today it is a symbol of the Resurrection, and of the Virgin Mary. However, our "Easter lily" is a comparative recent introduction.

One of the more common varieties in biblical times was the brilliant red Chalcedonecum Lily, somewhat resembling the modern tulip. Though the lily is mentioned many times in the Song of Solomon and other places in the Bible, we have no way of knowing just what variety is meant. Or even if, as in Jesus' reference to "the lilies of the field" (Matt. 6:28), other flowers might have been meant, such as the Field Anemone, which see.

LOCUST

LOCUST. The locust is the fruit of the Carob Tree, which see.

LOTUS

LOTUS. When we think of the lotus we very likely think of Egypt. There it was dedicated to Horus, god of the sun. The Hebrew people must have known of its pagan religious connotation. Perhaps because of it, the lotus never found a place in the symbolism of Judaism or Christianity. It is a water lily, found in many tropical and sub-tropical countries of the world.

LUPINE

LUPINE. The lupine, which grows profusely in the Holy Land, is almost identical with the variety familiar to our flower gardens. The blue lupine is most common, its striking color covering whole fields in Galilee in the late spring. An unusual characteristic is the handshaped leaves.

M

MALLOW. The mallow, found growing in swampy places in Palestine is very much like the thick, downy-leaved plant with which we are familiar. Its purple, pink and white flowers cover marshy areas. Though not too palatable the very poor sometimes use the think fleshy leaves for food.

MALLOW

MANDRAKE. A powerful narcotic, the mandrake has been used as an opiate since ancient times. It was also the basis of a "love potion." The creamy white flowers lined with purple give way to small pulpy fruit resembling small tomatoes in shape and color. The large heavy root is forked, and with a little imagination bears a resemblance to the human body. Probably this is why it is supposed to induce fertility. (Gen. 30:1, 14ff.)

MANDRAKE

MARJORAM. This is one of the smallest flowering shrubs in the Holy Land. Its shrublike stems are only a few inches in height, bearing clusters of white flowers among rocks and wall crevices. It belongs to the mint family.

MARJORAM

MINT. Mint of several varieties grows wild in the Holy Land. It is extensively used for flavoring. The Jews believed it efficacious in the treatment of many ailments. It was scattered over the floors of the synagogue, its fragrance scenting the air. Along with rue and cummin, mint was important enough to be tithed. (Luke 11:42.)

MINT

MORNING GLORY. The field variety of the Morning Glory grows over much of the Holy Land. The long trailing vine is quite often seen in the fields of grain, its pink and white blossoms coloring the grain stalks.

MORNING GLORY

MOUNTAIN LILY

MUSTARD

MYRTLE

MYRRH O.T.

MYRRH N.T.

MOUNTAIN LILY. Though not too abundant, this member of the amarylis family is found blossoming throughout much of the Middle East. It grows mostly in clay soil. The deep blue flowers are borne on foot high stems in clusters of three or four.

MUSTARD. Jesus knew whereof he spoke when he referred to the mustard seed as being "among the least of all seeds." (Matt. 13:32.) (Some seeds **are** smaller.) As he pointed out, it often grows high enough for birds to build nests in it. The yellow blossom variety is most common, but some kinds have white and lilac blooms. The ground seed furnishes the mustard of commerce.

MYRTLE. To the Egyptians, Greeks and Romans the evergreen myrtle was sacred and used in their worship. While not sacred to the Hebrews it was revered. The tent of the Tabernacle was covered with blooming boughs of myrtle. Isaiah mentions it as one of the trees that God "will plant in the wilderness." (Isa. 41:19.) And the familiar 55th Chapter of Isaiah closes with the promise that "instead of the brier shall come up the myrtle tree." Sometimes it is a bush, but again it may grow to be a 20 foot tree. The white blossoms are very fragrant and the aromatic fruits are dried for perfumes and spices.

MYRRH (O. T.). See CISTUS.

MYRRH (N. T.). The myrrh included among the three gifts which the magi brought to the Christ child was an aromatic made from the resin of the thorny, bush-like tree. The thick white gum which exudes when the bark is pierced, hardens on exposure to the air and becomes reddish in color. It has been used as a spice or as medicine since ancient times. The Hebrews used it as one of the ingredients of the anointing oil for the Tabernacle, and in the preparation of the dead for burial. Hence Nicodemus brought "a mixture of myrrh and aloes" to be sprinkled over the linen clothes with which he wound the body of Jesus. (John 19:39.)

N

NETTLE. The nettle of the Holy Land grows as high as 5 feet with nearly two feet of blooms on the flower stem. This height is indicated by Job when he berates those who have failed him: "Under the nettles they were gathered together." (Job 30:7.) It is a perennial, its spine-tipped leaves protecting it from marauders. Still, the lavender-streaked white flowers are beautiful —even if not gathered!

NETTLE

NARCISSUS. Our common pollyanna narcissus is one of the common spring flowers in Bible lands, growing profusely on the plains of Sharon and Jericho. It is quite generally agreed among scholars that this common but fragrant and beautiful flower is the "Rose of Sharon," which see.

NARCISSUS

O

OAK. The veneration of the oak by the ancients was not lost on the Hebrews. Mention of the fact that Deborah was buried beneath an Oak (Gen. 35:8) and that Gideon received "an angel of the Lord" under the branches of an oak (Judges 6:11) are instances that indicate it had a special significance. There are several varieties of the tree in Palestine, varying with the altitude and the soil. The expression "as strong as an oak" was as apt a simile when Amos recorded these words (Amos 2:9) as it is today.

OAK

OLEANDER. The tall oleander—it may grow as high as 20 feet—is one of the most beautiful shrubs in Palestine when in full bloom. The flowers cover a wide range of colors from white, rose, red to purple. They blossom in the spring and last all summer. It is an evergreen, easily grown. Unfortunately flowers and plant alike are highly poisonous; even the smoke from the burning leaves is wisely avoided.

OLEANDER

OLIVE. Asia Minor is believed to be the original home of the olive, which has been cultivated for thousands of years. It was an olive "branch" (twig) that the dove brought back to Noah on the ark. Jesus left the Upper Room and "went out unto the Mount of Olives." (Matt. 26:30.)

Olive trees have always been of practical value, the fruit for food, and the oil pressed from the fruit as oil for ancient lamps. And when Samuel took the horn of oil (olive) and poured it over the head of David to anoint him, he was following a ritualistic custom of his race.

OLIVE

ONION.

ONION. The onion, and its culinary cousin, the leek, was widely used for food even before biblical times. In the warm, dry weather of Palestine the cultivated onion grows very large and is very sweet. There are many wild varieties, some like the Pink Onion—the color of the blossom giving it its name—grows in rocky places to a height of 3 or 4 feet.

ONYCHA

ONYCHA. Mentioned with the sweet spices "stacte (storax) and galbanum" in Exodus 30:34, we know that the onycha was a source of aromatic resin from which is produced labanum. It is a 3 foot bush with large flowers having 5 white petals, each with a spot of scarlet darkening near the center and with stamens and pistil. Also known as the Rockrose, it blossoms profusely during the long dry season.

ORCHID

ORCHID. Orchids may seem out of place in the Holy Land and the familiar tropical species is not found there. But there are a dozen or more species that are common. The monkey orchid and the earth-wasp orchid are abundant in rocky soil. One of the most common varieties is the Antoilan orchid with rather small pink blossoms, several on a stem and of typical orchid shape. It blooms in March.

P

PANNAG

PANNAG. This is a variety of millet which, though not as palatable as wheat or barley, was extensively used for food among the common people, especially in time of famine. (Ezek. 4:9.) One stalk may produce thousands of seeds. They are hard and white and are ground into flour. (Ezek. 27:17.)

POMEGRANATE

POMEGRANATE. Growing wild in some sections of the Middle East, the pomegranate is a small tree with reddish bark, shiny green leaves and waxlike blossoms with crinkled, coral-red petals. The ripe fruit is about the size of an orange, maroon, with thick skin and many seeds. The juicy pulp is very palatable.

The popularity of the pomegranate is indicated in the fact that they were used as figures in the decoration of Solomon's temple (I Kings 7:18, 20). And pomegranate designs were braided into the hem of the ephod of the high priest. (Ex. 28:33, 34.)

POPPY. The poppy of the orient, the source of opium, was common in the Holy Land long before the Israelites settled there. The "gall" added to the vinegar and offered to Jesus (Matt. 27:34) was the juice of the opium poppy. This gesture may have been intended as an act of mercy since gall is a powerful sleep-inducing narcotic. The rather fragile lavender or white blossoms with a spot of purple at the base belie the sinister nature of the seed pod from which the opium is extracted.

POPPY

R

REED. One of the marsh plants common to the Middle East, the "reed" referred to in Ezekial 40:3 very likely was the variety "Phragmites." The stems of this reed were used for measuring. As with most similar plants, it grows to a considerable height, 12 feet or even more being not uncommon. The silky purple plume is often used for decoration.

REED

RESURRECTION PLANT. This plant, often available at our florists, is sometimes called the Rose of Jericho. When withered it closes into a ball, apparently lifeless and blown over the sands "like a rolling thing before the whirlwind." (Isa. 17:13.) Finding moisture, it sends out roots, unrolls and grows again. It is easy to see why the early Christians saw it as a symbol of immortality and considered it sacred.

RESURRECTION PLANT

RIE. In the plague of hail that fell upon Egypt, "the wheat and the **rie** were not smitten for they were not grown up." (Ex. 9:32.) A natural conclusion might be that **rye** was meant. But rie is correct. It is a grain closely resembling wheat though growing much taller and able to grow and produce in very poor soil. Though the rie flour was much inferior to that of wheat, it was extensively used, the two often being mixed, along with barley. (Isa. 28:25.)

RIE

ROSE. Wild roses are not too common in Palestine. The thicket rose, a dainty pink and white variety, climbs over the rocks of the hill country, blooming in the spring. A tall climbing variety with white blossoms grows in Galilee. The Phoenician rose, a tall bush species with clusters of single white flowers, grows in the higher regions of the Holy Land.

The "rose of Sharon" (Song of Solomon 2:1) is probably a poetic expression. Or it might have been the tulip, which see.

ROSE

RUE

RUE. One of the herbs which Jesus mentions in his denunciation of obeying the letter of the law only (Luke 11:42) was rue. It is a tall growing plant with clusters of yellow flowers with a knob of green. It was widely used as a disinfectant—its botanical Latin name means "strong smelling"—and also for medicinal purposes. Its strong, unusual taste apparently appealed to the ancients who used it as a falvoring.

RUSH

RUSH. There are many varieties of "rush" growing along the river banks and in the swampy areas of the Holy Land. Any one of these might be indicated in Bildard's query, "Can the rush grow without mire?" (Job 8:11). A common variety is the "Bob Rush," a grasslike plant growing over 4 feet high. The leaves are long and slender, cylindrical in shape. They are widely used to make mats and baskets.

SAFFRON

S

SAFFRON. The lavender colored saffron resembles the crocus, though larger, and it blooms in the fall. In biblical times, as today, the orange stigmas are the source of the saffron of commerce which is used as a condiment, as perfume, a coloring ingredient and in medicines.

SALVIA

SALVIA. The "Jerusalem Salvia," though of the same botanical family as our familiar red salvia, is quite different in appearance. It has the characteristic square stem of the family, but the blossom stems are spaced so that the individual flowers stand out, resembling tiny orchids, rather than the spike of solid bloom we know. It is thought by some to be the source of the design for the seven-branched candlestick common to the Jews.

SILVERWEED

SILVERWEED. This humble plant grows along the dusty wayside, its silvery fernlike leaves pressed flat against the ground, its small yellow flowers giving a bit of color to its drab surroundings.

SMILAX. The Prickly Smilax of the Holy Land is a close relative of the smilax we know. The very small greenish-white blossoms appear in October and November, followed by brilliant scarlet berries. These remain on the branches which are used for decoration much as we use sprigs of holly and other berry plants.

SMILAX

SPANISH BROOM. Sometimes called prickly asparagus, the Spanish broom grows in the woods of all the countries of the Mediterranean area. It is a shrub, peculiar with its long grooved stems which are widely used for weaving nets and baskets. The bright yellow flowers along the stems somewhat resemble small orchids.

SPANISH BROOM

SPEEDWELL. The white and blue Speedwell is common throughout the Middle East. It is an early bloomer, 3 or 4 inches high, blanketing much of the otherwise winter-barren landscape in early February.

SPEEDWELL

SPIKENARD. The spikenard which the woman poured over the head of Jesus (Mark 14:3) was indeed "very precious." One pound of spikenard cost 300 dinarii, nearly a year's wages. The spikenard plant is odd in appearance. The lower stems have a hairy covering from which grow the flower stems and leaves. The blossoms are red with a sweet fragrance. But the perfume, for which the plant is best known, comes from the hairy stem. To preserve its fragrance, spikenard is still transported in alabaster boxes as mentioned by Mark.

SPIKENARD

STAR OF BETHLEHEM. This is a different plant than the Bethlehem Star (see page 43). Both do belong to the lily family. It is a spring blooming plant with white six-petaled flowers on the end of 6 inch stems. The bulb is sometimes roasted for food or ground into flour. It is strange that such a lovely flower should be called by the rather inelegant name used in II Kings 6:25— "dove dung."

STAR OF BETHLEHEM

STYRAX (also STORAX). The white clusters of drooping white flowers of the styrax are very fragrant. They appear in March or April. The styrax is a shrub that may grow as high as 20 feet on the hills around the Jordan. It is especially abundant in Galilee. It is revered by the Palestinians, so much so that it is almost a calamity if one is cut down. Legend says that Moses, on leaving Egypt, made his staff of the styrax. Resin from the plant is used in medicine.

STYRAX

SYCAMINE. This is the Black Mulberry tree, the fruit closely resembling large blackberries. Familiar to the Hebrews while in Egypt, it is also known in the Holy Land. Jesus referred to the sycamine tree that "faith as a grain of mustard seed" could move. (Luke 17:6.)

SYCAMINE

SYCOMORE. About the only resemblance to this tree and the sycamine mentioned above is the spelling and the pronunciation. Both are mentioned in the New Testament which accounts for some of the confusion when one or the other is mentioned. The sycomore is a variety of fig of very poor quality. These grow close to the boughs and trunk of the tree. The large trunk separates into several branches quite close to the ground, making it easy for Zacchaeus to climb the sycomore tree that he might better see Jesus. (Luke 19:4.)

SYCOMORE

T

TAMARISK. Possibly influenced by the fact that it was sacred to the Arabs, Abraham planted a tamarisk tree at Beersheba. (Gen. 21:33.) It is a small evergreen with white flowers, flourishing in areas of very low rainfall. Thousands of tamarisk trees have been planted in the desert-dry regions, following the example set by Abraham.

TAMARISK

TARES. Jesus' parable of the tares in the wheatfield (Matt. 13:24-30) was so true to life that his listeners could not fail to understand his meaning. The plant referred to is bearded darnel, or rye grass. It so closely resembles the wheat plant during growth that it is difficult to tell the two apart until the grain heads appear, hence the point of Jesus' parable. Winnowing the grain blows away most of the lighter seeds of the tares. Any remaining are disposed of when the grain is shaken in a sieve, the smaller tare seeds falling through the mesh.

TARES

THISTLE. "Do men gather grapes from thorns or figs from thistles?" (Matt. 7:16). Jesus' listeners, quite familiar with the pestiferous thistle, must have smiled at the aptness of his question. Thistles are mentioned as early as Genesis 3:18, and often in the Old Testament. (I Kings 14:9; II Chron. 25:18; Hos. 10:8; Job 31:40, et al.) The downylike blossoms are lovely, but the stinging leaf hairs are their universal trademark.

THISTLE

THORNS. It is said that in no other country are there as many thorny plants as in the Holy Land. There are some 40 references to thorns in the Bible, many more if we include the often used synonym "brier." Since no plant names are given we can only conjecture which are meant in specific instances. It is natural that most interest centers around which one composed Jesus "crown of thorns." Many scholars believe it was the Paliurus, a common shrub growing from 3 to 9 feet high, bearing tiny white blossoms and with long, recurved thorns.

THORNS

THYNE TREE. John, writing from Patmos, mentions "thyne wood" among the merchandise that "the merchants of the earth shall . . . weep over." (Rev. 18:11, 12.) Also known as "citronwood," it is a conifer, resembling our arbor vitae. The fragrant wood was burned as incense and was highly prized for woodwork as it is almost industructible.

THYNE TREE

TULIP

TULIP. It is not strange to find the tulip growing wild in the Holy Land since it is native to nearby Persia. The tulip common in Palestine blooms early in the spring, as tulips do the world over. It is generally a striking red with pointed petals. It is quite generally believed that the tulip, growing profusely on the plain of Sharon, was the "Rose of Sharon" mentioned in the Song of Solomon 2:1. The literal translation of the original Hebrew word lends credence to this belief since it indicates that a bulb-growing plant was meant, not a shrub such as a rose.

V

VETCH

VETCH (Vetchling; Fetch). The Vetch, or Vetchling, of the Holy Land resembles our common variety. There, as here, its slender climbing stem grows in the fields of grain, attaching itself to the stalks. There are several varieties of vetch in Palestine. The "Charming Vetchling" is especially attractive with small orange-pink blossoms that look like sweet peas. Other varieties are blue.

W

WHEAT

WHEAT. Wheat is the most universal of all grains, so old that there is no record of when or where it originated. Keeping to the custom common today in most Europian countries, the English translators used "corn" where grain, including wheat, was referred to as was the case in Genesis 41:1, 5-7, when Pharaoh dreamed of seven full ears, then seven thin ears of "corn." Corn was unknown. But there was a variety of wheat with seven "ears" or heads of grain.

WORMWOOD

WORMWOOD. Wormwood is sometimes linked with gall (see page 50) as in Deuteronomy 29:18 and Jeremiah 23:15, an indication of its natural bitterness, especially the leaves which are used medicinally. It is a small shrub with small buttonlike yellow flowers.

OTHER ILLUSTRATED BOOKS IN THIS SERIES

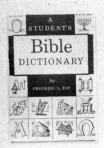  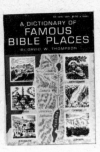 

A STUDENT'S BIBLE DICTIONARY, by Frederic L. Fay. A Student's Bible Dictionary sheds facts and light on many unfamiliar words and phrases commonly used in the Bible. Prepared for young Bible Readers, it is intentionally selective rather than all-inclusive. It contains special features of: 64 pages, paper cover, 795 word definitions, 264 drawings, and is handsome in appearance with clear, easy-to-read type.

A BIBLE WHO'S WHO, by David W. Thompson. A Bible Who's Who is a selected 64-page listing of over 600 people of the Bible with condensed biographies. 244 drawings. With each person there are: self-pronouncing helps, indication of Old or New Testament, male or female and scriptural references. The last four pages list the people in their order of appearance in the Bible.

A DICTIONARY OF FAMOUS BIBLE PLACES, by David W. Thompson. This book lists over 350 of the villages, cities, rivers, mountains, etc., in the Bible and a brief summary of their location and their contribution to the main stream of the unfolding drama of Bible life and history. 204 drawings add to the pictorial value of the book. 10 pages of useful maps and map meanings are also included.

A MAP BOOK FOR BIBLE STUDENTS, by Frederic L. Fay. The maps on the left hand page in this new Map Book show where the towns, cities and journeys were in the Bible narratives, and the accompanying text on the opposite page gives much helpful explanation and background material, as you read from the Bible itself.

ART STUDIES IN THE LIFE OF CHRIST, by C. Fraser Keirstead. This book consists of one hundred and sixty interpretations of our Lord's ministry, by seventy-six art masters. Each painting is reproduced, accompanied by facts explaining its composition and the Scripture it portrays.

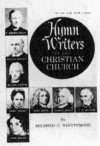

HYMN WRITERS OF THE CHRISTIAN CHURCH, by Mildred C. Whittemore. Here in brief form for quick reference is vital, interesting, and often little-known information concerning 181 hymn writers found in our leading hymnbooks. This is not the story of hymns, but of hymn writers. This book offers a picture of every hymn writer mentioned. This special feature is the only collection of such pictures in print.

Each Book Has 64 Pages

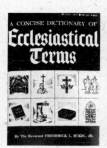
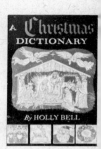

SYMBOLS OF THE CHURCH. Over 300 symbols with interpretations. Sections on the Old and New Testaments and the Saints. Also included are a Glossary of Ecclesiastical Terms, the meaning of Liturgical Colours, Forms of Clergy Salutations, and a complete index. Here in this attractive compact 64-page book is one of the most comprehensive and authoritative treatments in the field.

My First Book of Christian SYMBOLS. An interesting, instructive collection of 30 full-page sized symbols of the Christian Church with the story of their meaning and origin. Each page pictures one symbol in large outline form; on the back of each page is the complete story of that symbol. Perforations make it possible for each page to be removed and used as a flash card, story card or color card.

A Concise Dictionary of ECCLESIASTICAL TERMS, by The Reverend Frederick L. Eckel, Jr. An unusual volume featuring more than 600 ecclesiastical terms and their concise meanings taken from the traditions of the Church of England, Protestant Episcopal Church, and other of the larger denominations such as Baptist, Congregational, Methodist, etc. Profusely illustrated with over 200 drawings.

A CHRISTMAS DICTIONARY, by Holly Bell. Features a myriad of facts, stories, customs, carols, and poetry with over 200 fascinating spot silhouettes. The range is wide: from the birth of Jesus to St. Nicholas and Santa Claus; from medieval carols to "Twas the Night Before Christmas." Of universal appeal for any age group.

STORIES OF THE CHRISTIAN HYMNS, by Helen Salem Rizk. Tells the dramatic events behind the writing of 180 of Christianity's favorite hymns and gospel songs. It is a unique collection filled with interesting and vital information profusely illustrated with 180 line drawings bringing to life every hymn story.

WHO'S WHO IN CHURCH HISTORY, by John W. Brush. A concise volume featuring brief biographies of 240 leaders and thinkers of the Church from the early Christian centuries to the present era, and the contribution each has made to the story of Church History. Over two years were spent in search of pictures; and we are proud to say that an authentic reproduction of each person (240 pictures) is an unusual and dramatic feature of the book.